IT CAN'T BE TRUE!

Illustrated by *BILL TIDY*

Written by *JANE REID*

First published in Great Britain
in 1983 by

Octopus Books Limited
59 Grosvenor Street
London W1

Text and illustrations © 1983 Hennerwood
Publications Limited

Third impression, reprinted 1984

ISBN 0 86273 089 9

Made and Printed in Great Britain by
Richard Clay (The Chaucer Press) Limited
Bungay, Suffolk

IT CAN'T
BE TRUE!

CONTENTS

Legal Action

..................Being matters of a legal or
criminal nature..

No Christmas

In 1649 when Britain was ruled by Oliver Cromwell and his Roundheads, a law was passed abolishing Christmas and declaring that it should be an ordinary working day, like any other. People, however, thought that the Puritans had gone too far and continued to celebrate as usual. Many congregations were arrested in their entirety for doing so, but the law was soon repealed and Christmas became Christmas once more.

Prison Pottery Classes

The governor of a Northamptonshire prison was very pleased with the success of the pottery classes that he inaugurated. He even went along occasionally to watch batches of pots going into the kiln. What he didn't know was that one of the prisoners had become so good at moulding and firing that he was able to pass his work off as that of a famous potter. So good were his forgeries that they even fooled the experts at famous London auction houses. So much for retraining!

Just A Reminder, Sir

At Saltcoats, in Scotland, a man has had thirty letters and several visits from Post Office staff, reminding him that he does not have a licence. As he says, 'Why should I have a television licence? I don't have a television.'

★   ★   ★   ★

. . . . *A Dallas under-cover policeman began to chat up an attractive but obviously provocative girl standing in a dimly-lit alley way. The girl suddenly slapped a pair of handcuffs on him. She was in the same job as he was. . . . . . .*

★   ★   ★   ★

A Well-Judged Remark

F. E. Smith, who later became Lord Birkenhead, was a barrister of international repute. During one trial he referred to one of the witnesses as 'being as drunk as a judge at the time of the offence,' implying that his evidence was therefore not to be taken seriously.

At this point the judge interrupted and told Mr Smith that he believed the expression was not 'as drunk as a judge', but 'as drunk as a lord'. On hearing this, Mr Smith bowed to the court and said, 'As your lordship pleases.'

I Was Trying To Get Back In

Authorities at a well-known London prison had to confess that a press report that stated that prisoners were taking it in turns to slip out of the gaol at night to have a drink in one of the local pubs, much patronized by the criminal underworld, was, indeed, true.

The matter came to light when police arrested one prisoner climbing up the wall trying to get back inside after a night's illegal revelries.

Nothing Smashed, Nothing To Grab

Brighton, the famous English seaside resort, is also the home of a bustling antique trade.

There are several streets filled with such shops, all boasting attractive window displays of valuable *objets d'art* and jewellery. Naturally there are many attempts, some successful, to break into the shops.

In 1981 one would-be raider attempted a smash and grab raid on one shop. It was a pity for him that the shop owner had had the foresight to have specially reinforced glass put in. The brick the robber threw bounced back off the glass and knocked him unconscious.

Stay Granted

An Arizona sheriff was convinced that a man awaiting execution was innocent of the crime with which he had been charged and found guilty. He wired the Governor requesting a stay of execution and was greatly relieved to receive the following wire:

> STAY GRANTED STOP SIGNED H. SMATHERS, GOVERNOR.... BY E. RANDALL, TEMPORARY GOVERNOR.

It arrived a few hours before the execution was due to happen. The accused man was later proved to be innocent. What the sheriff did not know was that the telegraph operator who received the wire, appreciating the urgency of the situation, had taken the wire to the Governor's office in person, only to be told that he was terribly ill and could not see anyone. So the operator sent off the wire, having first signed it in his own name.

The Revenue's Revenge

In 1980, a woman wanted to register her 'practice' as a company.

The London-based Registrar of Companies was happy to accept her definition of the business as a provider of personal services. (The woman's services are those advertised as 'teachers' in the notice boards of seedy London newsagent shops.)

However, she desired to be more frank in the description of her business, and when the registrar refused, took him to court. The case was widely reported and the verdict went against the plaintiff.

Many people think that any publicity is good publicity, but one report of the proceedings caught the eye of the Inland Revenue who sent an inspector round to visit her premises. So, as well as having lost her case against the Registrar, the woman was faced with a tax bill of just under £11,000.

Any Excuse...

One dark December evening, London police arrested a lady of ill-repute and she was charged with soliciting. She asked to be released on the grounds that she was getting married the next day and had been out trying to earn some money to buy her husband-to-be a wedding present.

★ ★ ★ ★

. . . . .Duelling in Paraguay is quite legal, as long as both participants are registered blood donors. . . . .

BLAST...HIT HIS KIDNEY DONORS CARD!

An Escalating Battle

A Leeds postman was putting the finishing touches to smoothing some cement when a neighbour's dog walked across it. The annoyed postman set about re-smoothing the cement when the dog did it again. This time, the man threw his trowel at the dog and then kicked it. Unfortunately the kick landed on the wife of the dog's owner.

The incident was seen by another neighbour who decided to call the police. She ran across to the local telephone box and had just dialled 999 when the furious dog-owner's wife who had also decided to tell the police pulled her out of the 'phone box. A scuffle ensued and both ladies fell into the cement.

At this point, the postman's mother-in-law decided to intervene and although she was 86, she joined the scrap in the cement, pulling the poor postmaster in with her. Then the dog-owner himself came out of his house to see what all the commotion was about. He too was pulled into the cement.

They were all arrested for breach of the peace – all that is apart from the dog who had started it all.

★   ★   ★   ★

. . . . .In New York City there is an old law that has never been repealed making it illegal for women to smoke in public. . . . .

★   ★   ★   ★

Happy Anniversary

The presiding officer in Leeds magistrates' court knew the defendant very well. It was the 500th time he had appeared in court on a charge of drunkenness. He had first appeared there in 1922. The magistrate decided to give the man an absolute discharge, and gave him another talking-to on the evils of drink. Two days later the same man appeared on the same charge. 'I was celebrating my 500th appearance in court,' he told the magistrate. This time he was fined 50p.

A Piece Of Positive Police Work

A climber in Glencoe found a camera wedged in an ice covered ridge. He had the film inside developed and handed the photographs and the camera to the police.

The police spotted a car registration plate in one of the snapshots and traced the owner of the car who lived in Cheltenham, Gloucestershire. He confirmed that it was his camera that he had lost eight months previously.

A similar story concerns a factory girl who lost a ring one day at work. She searched and searched for it but there was no sign of it.

She left the factory several months later. Eight months after that her ring was returned to her. It had slipped off her finger and gone into one of the pillows that she was stuffing.

The pillow was eventually sold.

The buyer, one night, felt something lumpy in the pillow and found the ring inside it.

Protest Against Pomposity

Most of the people in the courtroom in Rio de Janeiro thought it was a tremendous joke when the accused, Ricardo Forenza stood up in the dock to give evidence on his own behalf. He had been charged with malicious conduct, in that he had removed the soap from the men's washroom in the nearby local government building and substituted it with joke soap which made the washers' hands turn black.

He explained that he had been there to see the tax inspector about his tax return, and he had been so pompous that Forenza thought he had to do something to bring him down to earth.

The magistrate seemed to agree with Forenza and let him off with a warning about his future conduct. Minutes after leaving the courtroom, there was an awful smell of rotten eggs and the whole court had to be cleared.

Forenza was hauled back before the magistrate and confessed to dropping two stink bombs as he was leaving the dock.

His defence was that he found the court too pompous. This time he was fined £100.

No One Would Kill Him

During a case in Monaco in 1912 the judge
passed the death sentence on the accused who stood before
him. According to Monegasque custom an executioner was
brought in from France to do the job, but when he appeared he
asked for 10,000 francs in payment. The authorities said that this
was too much. The executioner refused to budge and went back
to France. No one in Monaco could be found to do the job, so
the execution was held up indefinitely.

Meanwhile, the condemned man had become quite
comfortable in jail. He was the only prisoner there and the cost of
guarding him night and day was beginning to mount up.

A delightful compromise was arrived at. The prisoner was told
that he could live in jail under minimum security if he promised
not to escape. In addition, he would be given a small allowance
to pay for his needs. The man agreed and lived in the prison,
being paid for the privilege, until he died thirty years later.

I Felt A Bit Peckish, Your Honour

A French robber broke into a house outside Paris in 1964. He went into the kitchen and opened the refrigerator where he found some of his favourite cheese. He then found some biscuits and three bottles of champagne. He was arrested the following morning, fast asleep in the spare bedroom.

Banned And Banned Again

An Essex man was disqualified from driving by magistrates at Southend Court.

A few minutes after he left court, he decided to risk driving illegally. Unfortunately, the magistrate who had banned him spotted him at the wheel.

The unfortunate driver had to reappear in court where he was fined £300.00 and banned for another year.

Look, No Hands

A Brentford man was fined £2.00 for careless bicycle riding. When he was arrested, he was riding without his hands on the handlebars reading a newspaper. 'It was,' he told the court, 'the only chance I ever get to read a newspaper.'

Stop Clipping

Frau Inge Bader's husband has an art studio in Vienna. He finds that the brushes on sale there are not fine enough for his style of painting, so he used to clip his wife's eyebrows to make fine brushes. She tried to stop him but he was insistent, so Frau Bader went to court and got an order restraining her husband's strange habit.

Let The Punishment Fit The Crime

In Monroe, California, two students were sentenced to walk for twelve miles. They had been found guilty of siphoning three gallons of petrol from a parked car, and the judge considered that four miles to the gallon was a suitable punishment.

Similarly, three football rowdies in the town of Burntisland in Fife were ordered by the magistrate to report to the local police five minutes before kick-off time and five minutes after the final whistle as punishment for a breach of the peace during a Dunfermline–Raith Rovers match.

The gleeful youths had been expecting a much worse punishment and calculated that they could report at five minutes to three, be at the game (provided it was being played at home) five minutes after kick-off, and rush back in time to report, as ordered, five minutes after the final whistle.

They realized that if it was a cup tie, and the game went into extra time they would have to leave before the final result was known. However, they took no account of the canny Scots police sergeant who was on duty throughout their sentence.

They reported, as arranged, five minutes before kick-off the following Saturday. The sergeant told them to sit down and wait for a couple of minutes as he was 'a wee bit busy, at the moment.'

A few minutes later, they again asked the sergeant to clock them in and got the same reply. This went on for more than an hour.

Eventually, at half-past-four, ten minutes before the final whistle was due to be blown, the sergeant found time to log the boys' arrival at the station. He took his time doing so and they did not leave until twenty to five. Just as they were leaving, he called to them not to forget to report back in five minutes.

This went on every Saturday throughout the football season.

★   ★   ★   ★

. . . . Several tourists in Majorca have literally had the coats taken from off their backs by wily Spanish thieves, who, having told their victims that pigeons have soiled their clothes, help them off – permanently – with their jackets. . . .

I Swear By Myself...

A Florida man claimed against his insurance company when he was injured by the collapse of a pavement. The company dismissed his claims on the grounds that it was an Act of God, so the injured party decided to sue God and issued a writ against Him, claiming $25,000. The defendant did not appear in court, although a local priest offered to give evidence on his behalf.

Dual Nationality

A criminal in Venezuela owns a house that straddles the border between that country and Colombia. If ever the police try to arrest him, he simply locks himself in his bedroom until they go away. His bedroom is in Colombian territory, and he has been clever enough to keep a clean record there.

Not For Sailor's Use

Captain Cook, the great English explorer, worried about the possibility of scurvy breaking out among his crew. He knew that German sailors never suffered from it, a fact they put down to eating sauerkraut. But he knew that his sailors would never be forced to eat the German food, so he had a large barrel of it placed on the deck of his ship and placed an impressive sign over it:

FOR USE OF THE
CAPTAIN AND OFFICERS
ONLY.

During the day none of the sailors went near the tub, but every night the level of sauerkraut went down slightly and not one of his men came down with the disease throughout the trip.

17

What? Fisticuffs

An argument broke out during a conference being held in Richmond, Virginia. Tempers flared and when it was all over, one man had been shot dead and three others had been seriously injured. They were all members of the security staff from the Fifth Federal Reserve Bank who had been discussing ways of making employees safe from armed attack.

It's Hard To Give Up The Habit

The accused woman gained the sympathy of Swedish magistrates when she appeared before them on a charge of shoplifting. She was given a suspended sentence, but blotted her copybook almost immediately when she left the court, taking with her one of the magistrates' fur coats that she had found in the cloakroom. Her case was not so sympathetically heard on that charge!

What A Way To Serve A Summons

Police in La Paz, Bolivia had to serve a summons on a stilt-walking circus performer. To meet the conditions of the law, the summons had to be handed personally to him. However the circus man refused to come off his stilts to receive the legal document. Undeterred, the police went off, found some pairs of stilts and came up to his level to deliver the summons into his hands.

Mia Culpa

Father Giuseppe was a model priest to his 300 parishioners who respected him as a devout Catholic and friend. Imagine their shock when the good father landed in court, sued by the local baker for £5,000. Father Giuseppe was addicted to playing poker and had lost the money IN ONE NIGHT. His only possessions were a kitchen table and his bed.

Looks Familiar

A Newcastle family were on holiday in Spain. The caravanette was broken into and the mother's handbag and all the money that had been lying around was missing. They found the police very unhelpful – the Guardia Civil could find no one to speak English and the family spoke no Spanish. The municipal police told them that they were far too busy to deal with the case, but eventually agreed to take down details. Five days later the family was told that the handbag had been found, minus the contents. The woman went to the police station to collect it and was asked to sign for it. She didn't have a pen with her so she asked if she could borrow the policeman's. As soon as she saw it she recognized it as her own.

Quite A Haul

Marseilles police were cock-a-hoop when they announced that they had found a quantity of heroin worth £200,000 and had arrested an Englishman for possession. They later had to release him and confess that what they had thought was heroin was, in fact, a chemical freely obtainable from many chemists. Its use? To be dusted over areas in order to discourage dogs from relieving themselves.

HE'S NEVER BEEN THE SAME SINCE SNIFFING OUT THAT STUFF!

All Because Of A Car

Jerome Findley of San Francisco, an automobile dealer, disapproved of his daughter's choice of husband.

Findley was a highly-decorated former naval officer who had built up a successful business. He was conservative, both politically and in his way of life, and was a staunch Episcopalian. His prospective son-in-law was anti-war and had been a leading member of a punk group and a Roman Catholic, to boot.

Barbara, Findley's daughter, was adamant and eventually won her father's approval. Findley even grudgingly gave the couple a wedding present – a brand new Chevrolet, from his showroom. He did however lay down two conditions: one, that he would never set foot in his son-in-law's house and, two, that the couple should have dinner with him and his wife every Sunday.

Things were all right for several months, but then, one Sunday, Barbara telephoned to say that dinner was off as she had a bad ear infection, and had been advised to stay indoors by her doctor. She telephoned again, the following Sunday, and told her parents that she had not recovered. Findley and his anxious wife decided to drive over to see their daughter. Standing in their driveway was, not the Chevrolet, but a brand new Japanese Toyota.

Jerome took an automatic pistol out of his glove compartment and began to fire at the car. First he knocked out the headlights, then the windscreen and all the other windows. He then reloaded his gun and began to pump bullets into the bodywork.

Barbara's husband, Vincent, ran from his house armed with a shotgun and began to blast away at his father-in-law's Chevrolet. Before the police were called, several thousands of dollars' worth of damage had been done to both cars.

The distraught Barbara told police that they had traded in their Chevrolet for the Toyota to save money on petrol and had not known how to break the news to her father. But why had Jerome reacted so violently?

'A few months after the wedding my Chevrolet dealership was forced into bankruptcy,' he explained to the police, 'by the competition of a nearby Toyota dealer. I never liked my son-in-law from the start and the sight of that damned Toyota in his driveway was the last straw.'

Prisoner X

Many people have read *The Man in the Iron Mask* by Alexandre Dumas, about a plot to replace the King of France with his identical twin.

The fictional story is actually based on fact. In 1669, a masked prisoner was turned over to the warden of a prison in France. The prisoner had been sentenced to life imprisonment and was wearing a black velvet mask. He was to be allowed many privileges not enjoyed by other prisoners, and was forbidden to remove the mask.

He died in the same jail 34 years later, never having removed the mask, and his identity never having been revealed – even to this day.

Anyone Interested In A Little House At The End Of The Mall?

In 1923, Scotsman Arthur Ferguson convinced gullible American tourists that Big Ben and Nelson's Column were to be demolished and that he was responsible for trying to sell them on behalf of the British Government. He got £1,000 for Big Ben and £6,000 for Nelson's Column. He was so smooth-talking that he managed to talk one couple into giving him a deposit of £2,000 – for Buckingham Palace.

Stop The Vandals

Councillors in Queensferry, a small village outside Edinburgh, were fed up with the regularity with which windows at the local primary school were smashed by vandals, so they decided to build a wall between the school and the community centre where the young vandals seemed to spend most of their time. Builders got to work and when they finished work on the first day the wall was two feet high. When they returned the next morning they had to start all over again, because the vandals had knocked the wall down. All that was left was a pile of bricks.

I COULD RING BUGSY MALONE ON THE MOON BUT HE'S NEVER IN...

Freephone

Convicts at top-security San Francisco County Jail broke a code that allowed them to use the long distance telephone system operated by a company called MCI. By the time the authorities realized what was happening, the convicts had clocked up bills of over $100,000. One man was regularly calling a friend in South America. A spokesman for MCI said after the crime had been discovered that they were really grateful that the men had broken the system because they had had no idea that it was powerful enough to reach as far as that.

He Tried To Blackmail The President

Gaston B. Means got away with murder as well as being a spy, and an extortionist. In 1916 when he was a seedy little private detective on the surface, he was in fact spying for the German Kaiser, reporting British ship movements from the United States.
　　When America entered the war, Means persuaded the

Bureau of Investigation to hire him as a special agent. When in Washington he ingratiated himself into the good graces of rich people, often little old rich ladies. One of them was Maude King. Means hired thugs to attack her, and while the assault was taking place, he rescued her from her assailants. She was so grateful that she made him her personal manager. In this position Means had the chance to swindle her out of many thousands of dollars and when she noticed that her account was going down, she demanded an independent audit. Means said that he could see no reason why not and suggested a pleasant trip to the country to talk things over. During the trip, Mrs King had an accident with Means' gun and was killed. At least that's what he claimed and the coroner went along with his story.

In 1921 he was taken back by the Bureau where he kept a little black book detailing the sins and indiscretions of his colleagues. He managed to steal a diary of an Ohio poetess with whom the President, Warren G. Harding had been having a torrid affair for some time. Means offered it to the President and his wife for $50,000. Harding seems to have wanted to pay, but his wife was made of sterner stuff. She had Means kicked out of the White House. After the President died Means took his revenge, by publishing a disgusting little book accusing Mrs Harding of murdering her husband to hush up the affair.

Although J. Edgar Hoover was determined to get Means put away, the con-man was too clever for him. . . . He always chose his victims with great care. The nice little old ladies who were too incompetent in business to realize that Means was taking them for a ride, or young and beautiful ones who were too vain to admit that they had been taken in by him.

However he chose badly when he selected Evelyn Maclean as a victim. At the time of the notorious Lindbergh kidnapping case, he told the lady that he could get the child back intact, if only he had $100,000 to bribe some friendly bootleggers, who knew where the child was being held. Kind-hearted Mrs Maclean gave him the money in cash as he had requested.

The next time she saw Means was in court. She went to the police when she realized that she had been conned and the evil man was given eighteen years in jail. He died there, in 1938, with FBI agents clustering around his bed, trying to make him tell them where the money was.

He died with his wicked secret intact – and the money has never turned up.

Not A Very Neighbourly Neighbour

A Maryland man did not get on very well with his neighbours, in his home town of Glen Burnie. He had a minor dispute with three of them and whenever they passed his house he jumped out of his front door and shouted dirty names at them. The three neighbours took him to court where he was ordered to pay them $70,000 (£45,000) each. At just over £135,000 in total it was a very expensive row for the argumentative man.

A Ghostly Solution To A Ghastly Crime

Inspector Bhadule was sitting dejectedly in his office puzzling over the senseless killing of a pretty, 25-year-old schoolteacher. Suddenly a farmer from the nearby village of Kuhi, in the Maharastra area of India, came in and told the inspector that he knew someone who could tell him how to solve the case.

When the inspector asked the farmer who it was, he replied 'A ghost who insists on talking to you.' The policeman was understandably sceptical and dismissed the man; but he returned the next day and the day after.

The inspector decided that he had nothing to lose so with two local doctors to act as witnesses he went back to the farmer's village with him. The farmer took the three to a deserted field where stood the ruins of a temple.

When they arrived there the old man recited some mumbo-jumbo, blew a conch shell and called for the spirit to appear. Much to the astonishment of the sceptical inspector he heard a voice inside his head tell him where he would find the weapon that killed the girl.

The next morning the inspector went to where he was directed and dug. To his amazement he found a blood-stained knife and lab tests showed that the blood matched that of the victim. When the owner of the yard where the knife had been found was faced with the weapon, he broke down and confessed to the crime.

If you don't believe this, contact Inspector B. M. Bhadule at the police station in Maharastra in India and he'll tell you it's true.

Police...The Store's Being Robbed

In Frankfurt in 1979 three people broke into a department store. There were two men and one of the men's girlfriend. As they passed through the bedding department, the two lovers' desires became so strong that they passionately embraced on one of the beds there. Their embrace led on to rather more intimate things and the other man asked if he might join in. When he was told no, in no uncertain terms, he left the department, found a telephone and called the police to report that the department store was being broken into. Police arrived shortly afterwards and found the man and woman, literally with their trousers down. The caller had, naturally, left the scene of the crime but the arrested pair felt no sense of disloyalty at giving his name and address to the police.

★ ★ ★ ★

. . . . The citizens of Kentucky, USA, are required by law to take a bath once a year. At least they would be cleaner than King Louis XIII of France who had a grand total of five baths in his whole lifetime. . . . .

★ ★ ★ ★

Who's Sleeping In My Bed?

Golden Beach is an exclusive area in South Florida. Many rich and famous people live there and they hire security guards to ensure that their privacy is not invaded and to protect their homes while they are out of town. All the strict security did not deter a 29-year-old Canadian beach boy who simply dodged the guards, went up to the windows of the house of a wealthy Lebanese businessman, bent back the bars on a bathroom window, climbed in and looked around. He must have liked what he saw, for he stayed there for three weeks despite the gardeners and caretakers who were working in the grounds every day. While he was there he drank £900 worth of liquor, ate everything in the larder, most of what was in the freezer and ran up a £250 air conditioning bill. When the owner returned he found his uninvited guest fast asleep in bed – just like Goldilocks.

Talk Less Loudly, That's The Thing To Do

A New York businessman had to make a call from Chicago airport and asked the operator to put him through on his telephone credit card number.

When his wife got their monthly telephone bill she was horrified to see that it totalled $20,000 and most of the calls were to girls.

The man was shocked when his wife presented him with it on his return home. The bill ran to 334 pages and looked like a telephone directory.

After an investigation by the phone company it turned out that when he had quoted his credit card number over the phone, two marines in the next booth had overheard him and taken down the number. They had passed the number on to their buddies in the corps.

The unfortunate man had been paying to support the collective love life of half of the US Marine Corps.

Fortunately, he will not have to pay for the calls.

The Wild East

Train robbing Indians may, you probably think, belong to twentieth-century Hollywood movies.

You're wrong.

In India's rugged northern frontiers, bandits are holding up trains at an alarming rate.

In 1981 370 trains were robbed, 160 passengers were injured and 36 were killed.

The most common method is for a partner-in-crime to board the train as a paying passenger and pull the communication cord at some pre-arranged spot to allow gun-toting cohorts to board the train when it grinds to a halt. In other cases, bandits blow up sections of tracks to derail the trains – board them, pillage and make off with their booty.

So next time you're waiting for the 8.30, look at your watch, see that the train is 20 minutes late and curse, just thank the gods that you're not in India.

At Least The Police Didn't Put The Punters Away

Ladies of the night, who also work during the day, in and around the notorious squares of London's King's Cross district considered that they were being harassed by local police. The police claimed that the girls were operating outside the law and they were doing their job. Some of the ladies took over a local church hall by way of protest and created some publicity. The local council decided to appoint a monitor to protect the girls' interests. For her work she is paid £160 per week. The girls are most unhappy. Their trade fell off when the scheme was announced. 'After all,' said one, 'if a man is discussing terms he doesn't want someone standing over his shoulder taking notes.'

HAVEN'T HAD A CLIENT ALL WEEK BECAUSE OF HER!

Not On The Table

A group of Edinburgh golfers sat despondently in a bar in the small town of Gullane, a few miles to the east of Edinburgh and home of some of the best and most challenging golf courses in Scotland.

They had been looking forward to their game but the rain was coming down in torrents. After a few hours drinking one of them was rather the worse for wear, but suddenly the clouds cleared and the rain stopped. The others decided to play a few holes, but their companion was in no fit state, so they walked him back to their car, laid him across the back seat and left him sleeping peacefully.

An hour later they came back and there was no sign of their friend. They waited and waited, thinking that perhaps he had gone for a walk to clear his head, but there was still no sign of him.

They were becoming quite worried when a policeman came up to them and asked if they knew the driver of the car. When they said yes, the policeman told them that he was in the local prison on a charge of breaking and entering and gross indecency!

It turned out that he had woken up feeling a bit cramped on the back seat so he had decided to go for a walk. During his walk he had felt the need to relieve himself and being unable to find a public convenience had decided to ask at a house if he could use the lavatory.

There was no answer to his knock so he tried the front door. Being a small, quiet village the residents never bothered to lock the door when they went out. The man entered the house and searched for the lavatory, which he found.

He was unfortunately overcome with tiredness on his way out. So he lay down to sleep for a few minutes. He doesn't quite know how it happened but when the poor woman who owned the house returned she screamed when she saw the young man, lying completely naked on top of her dining room table.

After she had gathered herself together she telephoned the police who arrived within seconds and promptly arrested the still-sleeping man. He was fined £100 a few days later. The sheriff told him that in fining him so lightly he had taken into account several things including his age and background, which was very Edinburgh middle class. He was warned that if ever he was in trouble again, he would be punished much more severely.

The young man took the sheriff's words to heart; the next time he was in trouble he did not wait around to answer the consequences. He absconded with £10,000 of his employer's money and went to South America, leaving behind many debts – including £10 to the compiler of this book.

The Nails Gave The Game Away

Shortly after the First World War, the Frick Collection in New York paid more than $100,000 for a fourteenth-century carved wooden madonna.

In 1927 the carving was X-rayed as part of a routine check and was found to be a twentieth-century imitation. Investigations proved it to be the work of a man called Dossena who one day had sold a marble madonna to a man called Fasoli.

Fasoli, knowing it to be brand new, but also being a man with a criminal turn of mind sold it for a substantial profit. He contacted Dossena and bought more of his work and, unknown to him, sold it for more, passing it off as of antique value. Over the years Fasoli sold Dossena's work for more than £50,000 and paid Dossena next to nothing for it. One work which sold for $60,000 saw Fasoli pay the unwitting sculptor $600.00.

When all this came to light many museums had to admit that they had been fooled, but there was a vogue for Dossena's work and at an auction in New York in 1933 each buyer received a certificate from the Italian government that the purchase was an authentic Dossena forgery.

★　　★　　★　　★

. . . . When thieves broke into a church kitchen and stole two dollars, and cooked and ate five dollars' worth of hamburgers and two dollars' worth of ice cream, the local priest was a little upset at the theft but was pleased that the thieves had had the courtesy to wash up everything behind them. . . . .

★　　★　　★　　★

The Price Of Sin

Police in Tennessee, Illinois, were called to rescue a man who was trapped waist deep in the cess-pit outside a toilet by a local roadhouse. When they arrived he was almost dead. His body temperature had fallen to 91°F and he was unconscious. He claimed that he had been beaten and mugged by unknown attackers and thrown into the pit. At first the police believed him but became suspicious when they found his wallet, cheque book and credit cards lying in a neat pile in the men's room.

When asked about this the man confessed that he had been standing on top of the ladies lavatory roof watching through a 'glory hole' and had slipped and fallen into the pit. He had taken his personal possessions out of his pocket when he had gone to the men's room to wash, because, he told police, he liked to be clean when he went a-peeping and did not want to have anything on him to identify him in case he was caught.

Impractical Joke

Cincinnati citizen John Simon got rather too drunk one day and thought it would be fun to play a practical joke on a ten-year-old boy who was a common sight in the town, wandering around scraping a living by begging and selling pieces of crochet.

The boy was selling some crochet in the bar where Simon was drinking and the man told him that he wanted to buy one. He said that he was out of money and scribbled a note which he told the boy to take to the bank across the road.

The innocent boy did as he was asked and gave the note to one of the tellers. It was in fact a hold-up note and the teller pushed the alarm. The police arrived a few seconds later and promptly arrested the boy. He protested his innocence and took the police across the road to the bar where Simon was still sitting drinking. Simon found himself in court later in the week charged with malicious behaviour.

The judge, taking pity on the boy ordered Simon to buy him some warm clothes for the winter. Simon agreed to do so, but did not carry out the order. The judge had him thrown in jail and Simon very quickly found the money to buy the boy a splendid new winter wardrobe.

Allow Us, Sir

The Waldorf Astoria is among the grandest hotels in New York and is staffed with security men and detectives, among other, more usual hotel staff, whose job is to protect the wealthy residents who stay there. One night the hotel detective saw a man stumble as he came down the staircase into the lobby. In falling he dropped his suitcase which burst open and spilled out precious jewels all over the hallway. He summoned a porter and the two hotel men helped the grateful guest put everything back into the case, held the door open for him and hailed a cab... Only after the guest was safely away was the theft of more than half a million dollars' worth of gems reported to the desk clerk.

French Promises

At a dance in Foix, Aix-en-Provence, in France the band leader offered a prize of a television set to any woman who would remove her clothing. At first there were no takers, so he increased the offer to a television set and a tape recorder. This tempted one woman who stripped off in front of the assembled dancers. Police were not amused by the display and the woman found herself in court being fined 2,000 francs for immoral behaviour.

Unfortunately, the band leader was not forthcoming with the prizes and the poor stripper found herself with nothing at all for her labours.

31

The Religious Thief

A twenty-five-year-old burglar in Madras confessed to a string of robberies when he was arrested by police. He said that half of his loot could be found in the vaults of the temple of the Goddess Amman at Mangadu, near Madras. The police checked his story and found it to be true. When asked why he had donated half of his loot to the goddess, Venka replied, 'I have to steal to live. But I was brought up to believe in donating half my income to the temple. And I am still a very religious man.'

No Escape For Manson

Charles Manson, the madman who masterminded the Hollywood murders, is, thankfully, in jail in California. When he was assigned to clean the prison chapel, his guards became suspicious when they spotted the chapel door ajar but could not open it because it was being held by an electric cord. Manson came out when the guards ordered him to do so, but there were some odd things lying on the chapel floor.

A search of Manson's cell astonished the prison authorities, for they found that Manson was half-way through building a hot air balloon which he intended to use to escape from prison. He had simply written to a do-it-yourself balloon manufacturer and bought a kit by mail order. No one in the prison had bothered to check the package when it was delivered.

Only An Irishman (Sorry)

An Irishman toured dole offices all over Wales and southern England and claimed Social Security payments, using 24 names. The swindle netted him more than £500. He was eventually arrested and pleaded guilty of obtaining in one case £97 and in another £74 by fraudulent claims. He asked for eleven other offences to be taken into account. An inquiry revealed that if he had used his own name and made legal claims over the same period of time, he would have been legally entitled to £800, over £250 more than he had obtained fraudulently.

Arrested For Sweeping Up

A little old lady who lives in a small town in New York State liked the stretch of pavement in front of her house to be clean and tidy, and although the streets were cleaned by town authorities their work was not to her satisfaction. So, first thing every morning for ten years she got out her broom and set to work. The sidewalk was always scrupulously tidy. Until one day a new policeman was patrolling her area and saw her standing in the road sweeping rubbish into the gutter. He promptly gave her a ticket for jay-walking (a finable offence in the United States) and the eighty-two year old woman found herself in court. Fortunately the judge let her off – but only after making her promise to sweep the pavement without standing in the road. He didn't, he said to her, want to see such a public-spirited old lady as herself get knocked down and injured.

Black Market Money

Kevin Butler was an ordinary London mini-cab driver, whose radio-linked cab drove around North London picking up fares. One day he took a Nigerian businessman, Kizoto Idehem to a bank and waited for him while he withdrew cash from his bank. The money was in a black bag which Mr Idehem laid on the back seat. He asked Butler to stop outside a shop and went in to buy something. He never saw Butler again. As soon as his back was turned, Butler drove off – with £241,000 belonging to the Nigerian. To date, he is still free.

★　　★　　★　　★

. . . . The man in the dock in a Scottish court looked shamefaced as his girlfriend claimed that he had hit her on the head with an axe, twice, while she had been lying in bed. Not satisfied with that, he then assaulted her with a can of soup. Having done so, the can was then opened and the couple warmed it and had it for supper. . . . .

★　　★　　★　　★

Mere Technicalities

.... *Being matters of a mathematical,*
statistical or technical nature...................................

Movable Months

In the Western world the month of December always falls in winter, but, because they use a different calendar, a Moslem month that occurs in winter one year will fall in summer thirty years later. Interestingly enough, it would be possible for a Moslem who converted to Judaism to celebrate his first birthday 4,340 years later. This is because of differences in the systems the two faiths use to calculate the year. Moslems calculate the year from the date of Mohammed's flight to Mecca in 622 (in the Christian calendar). Jews calculate the year from the time when they believe the world was created – 3761 years BC. Therefore 1982 is 1403 to Moslems (if you decide to work that out, you must remember that the Moslem year contains only 354 days!) and 5743 to the Jews. Complicated, isn't it?

I'm Millions Of Thingies Tall

The smallest unit of measurement is called the attometre. It is only used in the microest of micro calculations and is so small that you could never see anything one attometre long. The average human thumb is 7,000,000,000,000,000,000 attometres long – and that's an awful lot of attometres.

★　★　★　★

. . . . $11,111,111^2$ *equals* **123456787654321**. . . . .

★　★　★　★

News Travels Fast

If a rumour was started at midnight and repeated within two seconds by everyone who knew about it to two people and those two people told two people and those two people told another two people ... everyone on earth would know about it by 6.30 in the morning.

Underground Wonder

In 1900 a Sicilian immigrant entered the United States, penniless, although he came from a wealthy family. He had been disinherited after a family quarrel. He worked hard as a farm labourer and eventually saved enough money to buy a piece of land on which he intended to build a house for himself and the girl he intended to marry.

The land, however, turned out to be a barren piece of rock with a small wooden shack on it. The man decided that it was too hot to live in the shack, so he built an underground cellar where he could go to cool off. The cellar was so successful that he built another room adjoining it. Then he added a kitchen, hallway, bedrooms and a library.

The rooms were lit by natural light let in by fanlights sunk in from above and there was even an air conditioning system based on a ventilation duct that brought cool air up from below. There was also a garden, again lit by a skylight, which is still, today, filled with exotic plants and shrubs.

However, he took so long about building it – 39 years to be exact – that his fiancée got fed up and ran off with another man. The heart-broken man died alone in his underground palace in 1946.

A Shortage Of Hotel Space

The Japanese, pioneers of miniature radios and electronic gadgets are also the pioneers of miniature hotel rooms.

Building space in Asaka is at such a premium that a new hotel has been built which contains 411 sleeping capsules, each equipped with a reading light, a television set, radio and transistor radio and digital alarm clock.

The 'rooms' are three feet high, thirty inches wide and six feet deep.

Every capsule has been filled every night since the hotel was opened in 1979, mainly by businessmen who have been out drinking and have missed their last train home.

Square Earth

Apart from a few people who still believe that the Earth is flat, everybody believed that the Earth was round – until photographs taken from American space shots proved that actually it is pear-shaped. Recent research has, however, shown that the Earth in fact has four CORNERS, one in Ireland, and three in the oceans near Peru, South Africa and New Guinea. It really is a square world after all.

★   ★   ★   ★

. . . . If the 4½-billion-year history of the Earth were to be measured in proportion to one year, man did not appear until 8.30 pm on December 31. . . . .

Enter A Different World

Harrods, one of the smartest shops in London, has always prided itself on caring well for its customers – pandering to their every need. In 1898 Harrods installed the very first escalator in Britain in their Knightsbridge store.

But in case any of their wealthy customers found the moving staircase too much for their nerves, liveried attendants were positioned at the top to offer smelling salts or brandy to anyone who wished it.

We do not know how many customers went straight back down and up again ... and again ... and again ...

Hoot Mohammed

Bagpipes, which are associated with Scotland more than any other nation did not originate in that country. They were first played in Persia hundreds of years before the Scots first played them, and spread from there to many parts of Europe. Many people probably wish they had stayed in Persia.

The Drachma In The Slot Machine

Machines operated by coins, such as cigarette machines or chocolate dispensers are, you may think, a twentieth-century invention. Well, you would be completely wrong. Nineteenth century? No. Eighteenth? No.

Slot machines were actually invented by a Greek scientist called Hero, in the first century AD.

Holy water was sold in temples. The water was contained in urns with a short pipe leading out from the base. The top end of the pipe, inside the urn, was closed by a plug which was fixed to one end of a horizontal bar.

The other end was directly underneath an opening where coins could be inserted. When the coin dropped in, it hit the end of the bar and caused it to move down. This caused the plug to open and the holy water to trickle out.

A Good Banking Service

The Bank of England, in London, has a special department that deals with claims for reimbursement of ruined banknotes. One of the most common causes of damage is – washing machines! Long-forgotten notes still line the pockets of many a dirty pair of trousers, and emerge from their ordeal clean but unusable. Other culprits are dogs, and lawnmowers, but there have been a few really weird claims.

One Church of England vicar tore up a fiver during a sermon to demonstrate the worthlessness of money, and then filled in a form claiming the money back from the Bank. A magician borrowed a pound note from a member of his audience and put it into a shredding machine, assuring the lender that it would be all right. The trick failed and the conjurer sent the shredded money to the Bank and was reimbursed.

One family whose house was broken into found that their safe had stood up well to the heat of the robbers' acetylene torch. But the heat had been so intense that the cash inside had burned. The charred remains were sent to the Bank and the family got their money back.

In 1981 the Bank paid out £607,890 in this way.

★   ★   ★   ★

. . . . *Mount Everest, at 29,000 feet, is one foot higher than it was one hundred years ago. The earth's forces that created it are still working.* . . . .

★   ★   ★   ★

A Shaving Success Story

In 1895 King C. Gillette had a wonderful idea. He was fed up with having to use a cutthroat razor every morning so he set about designing a wafer thin, incredibly sharp blade that could be held together by a safety clamp. It took him eight years to perfect the design and when it went on sale in 1903, he thought he had been wasting his time for in that year only 51 razors and 168 blades were sold. The following year, however, he knew it had been worthwhile. 90,000 razors were sold and *12,400,000 blades*.

40

France To England — By Horse And Coach

Several French and British governments have studied the feasibility of linking the two countries by means of an underwater tunnel. The last one, which was abandoned in 1974, would have cost £846 million. But work was actually started on the digging on an earlier project in 1881. The tunnel is still there. The workers dug a tunnel, seven feet high and 879 yards long, from Kent out under the Channel. The idea was to link Dover with Calais and to transport people between the two in horse-drawn carriages along the candle-lit passageway. Work was abandoned shortly after it had begun.

★   ★   ★   ★

. . . . .The average human being produces two to three pints of saliva every day. That is almost 8,000 gallons during the course of an average life. . . . .

★   ★   ★   ★

Spring Will Be A Little Early

The Russians have a novel way of making snow melt earlier than it would normally. When the first weak spring sunshine appears, they spray the solid snow fields with coal dust. The black dust absorbs more heat than would otherwise get to the snow, so it melts quickly.

Dry Lakes

Oklahoma legislators decided to build several new reservoirs and ordered the state cartographer to redraw tourist maps with large blue splodges where the lakes were planned to be. Unfortunately funds ran out before the first lake was completed so motorists who drive out to the country expecting to be able to picnic beside an attractive lake are met with barren, bone-dry basins.

Better Late Than Never

The Camden librarian opened the letter on his desk and read:

I suggest that all those disgusting books by Mr Havelock Ellis and other similar dirty-minded men posing as psychiatrists be removed from your shelves. Nay sir, I do more than suggest it – I demand it! You are contributing to the undermining of the fibre of the English people – and if war comes, we shall be in no fit state to wage it.

Mr Cole, the librarian, received the letter in 1977. It had been posted in 1938, one year before World War II broke out.

A Crowning Achievement

An American scientist asked several people to identify the subject of a photograph he had taken in 1937. Most of them said that it was an elaborate hat or a crown. In fact it was a drop of milk splashing into a bowl, which he had photographed at a flash exposure of 1/10,000th of a second.

★   ★   ★   ★

. . . . *If all the telephone lines under New York City were straightened out, they would reach from here to the planet Venus.* . . . .

★   ★   ★   ★

Small Is Beautiful

Most people have heard that the Lord's Prayer can be, and often has been, written on the back of a postage stamp, but how many know that microfilm technologists in Dayton, Ohio, have put every book in the Bible on to cards 1 inch square? Each book can be read quite clearly under a microscope.

Perhaps even more miraculous is a new Japanese camera that is 1.14 inches long and 0.65 inches thick.

Amazing What A Body Can Make

The human body contains enough iron to make a nail, enough carbon to make the lead of 9,000 pencils, enough phosphorus for the heads of 2,000 matches, fat for seven bars of soap, as well as three pounds of calcium and one ounce of salt.

Blue Moon

In 1883 after the volcanic eruption at Krakatoa, near Java, so much dust was thrown up into the atmosphere that the moon appeared to be blue in the night sky. The dust scattered the light which became richer in short wavelengths, thereby intensifying the blue light.

Just To Make Sure

William Dewer's mother-in-law was not at all impressed when he showed her his new invention – the vacuum flask. It would, he assured her, keep things at a constant temperature for hours. Not only did she disbelieve him, but to make sure that the one he gave her worked effectively, she knitted a woollen cosy to fit over it and retain heat.

Power By Rubbish

Nashville, Tennessee City Council collect lorry loads of rubbish from the city tip every day and feed it into an incinerator boiler where it is burned and converts water into high-pressure steam. The steam is used to spin the rotors of a turbine which generates enough electricity to provide heat and air conditioning for 38 office blocks.

The plant cost £6.8 million to build in 1974, and paid for itself within a year.

★ ★ ★ ★

. . . . Office space in central London is now so expensive that it costs £50 a year to rent the space taken up by an average wastepaper basket. . . . .

★ ★ ★ ★

A Sweet Victory

Scientists who developed the limpet bomb during World War II came up against a serious problem that threatened to jeopardise its success.

No matter what chemical they tried they could not find one that dissolved at a constant rate in both salt and fresh water, which was essential to activate the trigger mechanism.

Then one of the scientists had a brainwave. He tried it out and it worked. The magical chemical – ordinary aniseed, exactly the same as is used to make aniseed balls.

It's Worth About Ten Pounds!

In 1886 a South African gold prospector sold his claim in the Transvaal for the equivalent of ten pounds.

Ever since then, the mines that have been sunk there have realized seventy per cent of the Western world's total gold supply.

Talk about being short changed.

Stretching A Point

If all the tiny tubes in the human kidney were stretched out and laid end to end, they would run for forty miles. (In similar vein, Dorothy Parker once said that if all the debutantes in Yale were laid end to end she would not be at all surprised.)

A Few Surprising Facts In The Day In The Life Of The World

Every day your heart pumps enough blood to fill the fuel tanks of about 400 cars. The population of the world increases by about 200,000. Nine million cigarettes are smoked. 740,000 people fly off to foreign countries. International trade brings in $1.5 billion. Enough water evaporates from the oceans to fill five million average sized swimming pools. In America 10,000 serious crimes are committed and in Japan twenty million commuters cram into trains. In Russia 1.3 million telegrams are sent. 20,000 aircraft take off carrying almost one and a half million passengers and fly a total of 13 million miles. 200,000 tons of fish are caught and 7,000 tons of wool are sheared off sheep. Enough tobacco is produced to give everyone in the world two cigarettes and the equivalent of 23 million tons of coal is burned to produce energy.

Read It Quick

By the time you have read this paragraph (assuming that it will take you about half a minute) 50 people will have died and 120 will have been born. The human population increases at a rate of 140 per minute.

★   ★   ★   ★

. . . . *Eskimos use refrigerators. Not to keep food fresh as we do but to prevent it from freezing solid, as it would if left outside in the ice and snow of the Arctic.* . . . .

★   ★   ★   ★

A Dream Come True

A Colombian priest dreamed that his little flock of men and women would one day have their own cathedral to worship in. The town was poor and most of the people in the parish were employed at the local salt mine, the largest salt producer in the world. Eventually his dream came true. It took six years to build the Cathedral of Our Lady of the Rosary. It can seat 5,000 worshippers. Its nave is 400 feet long and 73 feet high. It is supported by columns 33 feet square. Outside there is parking space for 200 cars. The cathedral is built entirely of salt and is 800 feet down the mine beneath the summit of the salt mountain. It is reached by a deep tunnel more than one mile long.

A Fishy Story

If a man or woman wants to gain one pound of weight by eating fish, more than one thousand pounds of other living things must die first. The person would have to eat ten pounds of fish, which in turn would have to consume one hundred pounds of small fish creatures, which would in turn have eaten more than one thousand pounds of plankton.

Hot Stuff

There are several authenticated stories of unfortunate people spontaneously combusting. One gruesome photograph shows all that remains of one poor man who burned to death in his bathroom – his calliper. Experts are puzzled by the phenomenon.

They reckon that the heat necessary to destroy the human body so completely is 3,000°C and the heat is always localized in the part of the room in which the combustion takes place. The fire never spreads.

Pity therefore the poor young man who was dancing with his fiancée at a disco in Chelmsford. Suddenly, in front of the horrified assembly, she burst into flames in her fiancée's arms.

Travelling Theatre

The Royal Exchange Theatre in Manchester is one of the most famous companies in Britain. The stage there, in the 700 seat theatre, is such that the plays are always performed in the round. This makes it difficult for them to take their productions on tour, but the demand for them to do so has been so great that they have designed a portable aluminium structure which, when erected, can take a stage the same size as the original, seat 400 people, and use the complete lighting and sound systems as used in the original productions. When it is dismantled, the theatre can be packed into TWO lorries.

I Don't Want To Know

Shoppers in Stop and Shop, a grocery chain in Massachusetts gave the thumbs down to new cash registers which, when the total button was pressed, announced how much was due. The reason, according to a survey, was that shoppers did not want to *hear* how much they had spent, it was bad enough having to pay anyway.

Sheer Croppers

.... *Being matters of an accidental
or calamitous nature.......................................*

Stuck – By The Lips

A Lancaster driver returned to his car one day and found that the lock had frozen. Being a non-smoker he had neither matches nor lighter to defrost it, so he went down on his knees and breathed on it hoping that his warm breath would do the trick. It didn't. Instead he became stuck to the lock for twenty minutes!

A Fishy Tale

A 51-year-old company director was relaxing at home one evening while his wife was in the kitchen preparing their supper – a fine six-pound pike that her husband had caught six hours earlier on a fishing trip. Suddenly, he heard his wife scream. He ran into the kitchen and found her crying and trying to staunch a wound on her arm. The pike had bitten her as she lifted it up to clean it.

Such A Sad Waste

German stevedore Wilhelm Schmidt of Hamburg had never suffered or caused any accident during the 43 years he worked at the docks. On the day he retired, his workmates presented him with a case of whisky. Unfortunately it proved too heavy for him and he dropped it on his foot, breaking three toes.

One In The Eye For Justice

A customer of a certain fish and chip shop found himself in court charged with assaulting the owner. It seems that as he was queuing for his supper, he sneezed and his glass eye shot from its socket into the hot fat-filled deep frier. The owner was forced to drain the tank and clean it. He picked out the eye with a pair of tongs and threw it on the floor. This was too much for its unfortunate owner who promptly leaned across the counter and slapped the owner's face.

Smoking's A Headache

An American soldier was accidentally shot through the head while serving in the army. Surgeons removed the bullet but could not sew up the hole in his brow. The unfortunate man lived for many years with this hole, through which he could blow out cigarette smoke.

Suicidal

A New York painter decided to end it all by throwing himself off the Empire State Building. He took the lift up to the 86th floor, found a convenient window and jumped. A gust of wind caught him as he fell and blew him into the studios of NBC Television on the 83rd floor. There was a live show going out, so the interviewer decided to ask the would-be suicide a few questions. He admitted that he'd changed his mind as soon as he'd jumped.

★　　★　　★　　★

.............'Of course the water's safe to drink,' said English novelist Arnold Bennett in Paris one day in 1931. He promptly drained a glass of unboiled water, caught typhoid and died. . . . .

★　　★　　★　　★

A Hot Christening

Guests at a christening party in Peterhead near Aberdeen gasped in astonishment when the godfather of the child being baptized performed a spectacular rugby tackle on the priest in charge of the ceremony, brought him to the ground and pulled his vestments off him. What they had not seen, that only the godfather had noticed, was that the cleric's robes had brushed against a candelabra and flames were licking up his back. Everyone else had been doting on the baby and had not seen the fire start. The baby slept throughout the service, not waking up once.

Not Again, Pierre

Pierre Joilot backed his fork lift truck over the wharf edge at Toulouse Docks where he worked. His employers were understanding and took no disciplinary action against him. Not even the second time he did it, nor the third, fourth or fifth. However, after the sixth truck in two years went into the water, the unfortunate M. Joilot was dismissed.

A Cold But Fortunate Escape

Two fishermen were out one night in their 40-foot boat, when it was hit by a sudden storm and wrecked. They were found two days later, well fed and not too badly hurt. Their craft did not have a lifeboat, so when it went down they threw the refrigerator overboard and clung on to it as it floated along. When they were hungry, they simply opened it up and had a snack.

IF I EVER SEE ANOTHER FISH FINGER ...

Please Don't Do It Yourself, Darling

Tony Thompson is an avid do-it-yourself fan. One day, after watching plumbers install a new bathroom in his house, Tony decided to fit a shower curtain. Unfortunately, his electric drill slipped out of his hands and cracked the new porcelain sink. As he reached out to stop it falling he fell off the ladder. His hammer left a huge hole in the new bath and the ladder fell on top of the water closet, cracking the tank and several of Tony's ribs.

When he came out of hospital and was feeling ready for action again, he decided to remove an old fireplace. This went slightly better. Tony survived unharmed, but a sharp piece of flying concrete shattered the television set in the corner.

He then decided to paint his carport, so he tied his ladder securely to a window frame and set to work. Unfortunately, he slipped off and fell through a fanlight, covering himself and his car with a gallon of paint. As he fell he grabbed on to the window frame and pulled it right off the wall.

Undeterred, Tony decided to tile his hallway and bought some expensive Italian tiles for the job. He stored them at the foot of the stairs ready for work the next morning. But he slipped on his way down and smashed every one.

You'd think he'd give up, but no. Shortly afterwards he was drilling a hole under his kitchen sink. It's a pity that he forgot to empty it first. When the drill went through the sink Tony was covered in a torrent of dirty dishwater, and the drill blew up, almost electrocuting him in the process.

Fortunately, his wife understands his obsession and refuses to leave the house when he gets to work – she always hovers close by with the first-aid box in her hand – just in case.

Fore

The pilot of a plane taxiing along a runway in California suddenly collapsed over the controls and the co-pilot had to land the plane. The pilot's collapse was the result of a freak accident – he had been hit on the head by a golf ball struck on the adjoining golf course by someone who, I suspect, lost the hole.

Asleep On The Job

A Heathrow Airport baggage handler was in the hold of a Tri-star waiting for the last bag to be loaded. He lay down for a few seconds' rest and unfortunately fell asleep. When he woke up the plane had taken off. He cried for help and was freed by the flight crew, using a trap door that led from the baggage hold into the lavatory inside the plane. They led him to a seat and gave him a hot meal.

When the plane landed in Bermuda, the accidental passenger was put on the first return flight by immigration officials. He returned to London not just to face the ribbing of his workmates but also a bill for £298 from British Airways for the cost of the flight.

Killed – By A Fish

In the 1930s a Canadian angler fishing in one of the many Canadian lakes was delighted when he landed an extraordinarily large pike. He duly despatched it with a heavy stick and laid it down on the bank beside his shotgun. Unfortunately, the fish was not properly dead. It began to thrash about and its tail caught on the trigger. The gun went off – sending the angler to the happy hunting ground in the sky.

An Expensive Accident

Near the city of Bikaner, in Rajasthan, India there is a temple dedicated to the goddess of poets. The poets who are called Charans have a strange belief. The temple courtyard is a swarming mass of rats, around 100,000 of them.

The Charans think that when they die, they become one of the temple rats, and that when a temple rat dies, it returns to earth as a Charan poet. If one of the poets accidentally steps on a rat and kills it he is fined for his accident – an amount of silver equal to the weight of the poet to whom he has gone to pay his respects.

A Slight Headache

In 1955, *The Times* reported that a South African had been shot in the head. The bullet had entered the back of his head, passed through the lobes of his brain and come out above his eyes. The man walked to hospital and, apart from the flesh wounds, was found to be perfectly all right. He did have a headache.

★   ★   ★   ★

. . . . *The registrar at Toulouse General Hospital in France told the man standing in front of him that the hospital would be pleased to accept his body after death for medical research, whereupon the elderly gentleman shot himself. . . . .*

An Odd Accident

A Somerset man parked his car on a hill and went to a nearby telephone box to make a 'phone call. As he was in the box, another car swerved into his and released the handbrake. The man watched in horror as he saw his car come closer and closer and closer until finally it crashed into the telephone box and, with him still inside, knocked it over.

Trapped In The Loo

A sixty-year-old Liverpool woman decided that her bathroom needed cleaning. She set to work but had some difficulty in reaching the wall above the lavatory cistern.

She decided to stand on the rim of the lavatory bowl, so she put her bucket down, clambered and stretched her arm up. Suddenly, she slipped on the wet porcelain. Her right foot went into the bucket of water and her left plunged straight down the toilet. She fell backwards and her foot became trapped in the S-bend.

Try as she might, she couldn't pull it free and no one answered her cries for help. She eventually managed to remove her right foot from the bucket but could do nothing about her left one. Finally, one almighty yank did the trick and she hobbled round to her doctor who treated her for a badly bruised toe.

A Volcanic Romance

The Island of Reunion is the ideal place for a honeymoon. Tropical climate, balmy nights, romantic beaches – they can all be found there.

A young Frenchman certainly thought so when he took his bride there in 1977. They hired a honeymoon cottage and at first everything was quite perfect. One evening, however, the newly-married man decided to vault over the fence around the cottage and surprise his wife of three days. Unfortunately he had lost his way in the tropical darkness, plunged headlong into a crater of the Ganga Volcano and died.

An Expensive Loss

Prince Urussoff was an extremely rich Russian nobleman who was extremely superstitious as well.

While honeymooning with his bride on the Black Sea, her wedding ring slipped off her finger and disappeared beneath the waves.

The Prince believed, according to an old family superstition, that the loss of a wedding ring would bring about the death of the bride, so he bought both shores of the Black Sea, believing that if he owned the sea, he still owned the ring lying on the sea bed. He spent $40 million buying the shores.

But when he died, his family did not want the ring, so they decided to re-sell the Prince's property – and they got $80 million for it.

In Sickness And In Health

The guests at a wedding in Rochester, New York were sorry for the obviously still-recovering bridegroom when he was led to the front of the church to await his bride. They knew that he had been in an accident and was slightly concussed. They nodded sympathetically when the bride hobbled up the aisle, her foot in a splint because of a broken toe as a result of the same accident. The head bridesmaid, also in the accident, was sporting a black eye and limping slightly because of a sprained ankle. The other two bridesmaids each had an arm in a sling – one because of a fractured humerus and the other due to a dislocated shoulder: victims, not of the same accident, but of separate skating disasters.

★   ★   ★   ★

. . . . .In 1666 much of London was destroyed by a fire which started in a baker's shop in Pudding Lane and spread quickly, devastating building after building. Amazingly only six people died in the conflagration. . . . .

★   ★   ★   ★

Exploding Soup

An Aberdeen woman decided that the broth she was preparing needed some hot water added to it. She lifted her electric kettle, tilted it forward and – WHAM. She had forgotten to disconnect the plug from the kettle and as she tilted it, the live plug became free and landed in the soup. The soup went everywhere – even covering the ceiling. Somehow, she hasn't really wanted to make soup since.

Oh, What A Picture

A woman who lived in San Diego in California and some friends were having a fun day on a picnic. The girls were preparing the food and their boyfriends went off to do some target practice with their hand pistols. When they came back someone suggested taking a photograph and everyone lined up in front of the camera.

One of the men thought it would be a fun idea if he dropped his pants in the photograph. Unfortunately, as the pants hit the ground, the pistol in his pocket went off and struck the girl and his wife. The wife was furious with her husband, not only at the time of the accident, but a few months later when a judge awarded the girl $260,000 damages.

A King's Road Caper

A well-known newspaper editor was dining with some friends in a fashionable King's Road restaurant. The restaurant employed a violinist to move between the tables serenading the customers. One of the party saw that this was causing some embarrassment to a lady in the group, so he decided to tip the fiddler with a ten pound note, hoping that he would move on. He leaned back and without looking at what he was doing, tried to push the note into the violinist's pocket.

The guests watched with a mixture of hilarity and astonishment as he pushed and pushed, apparently having difficulty in getting the money into the pocket. Hardly surprising, he was trying to push it into the violinist's trouser fly!

HELLO, MRS. BROWN. HOW ARE YOU? I WONDER IF YOU'D MIND TELLING THE PRESIDENT...

ATTACK

Sorry, Wrong Number

A New York housewife in the 1960s had the same digits in her 'phone number as that of the White House in Washington. To make matters worse, the area code for New York is 202 and that of Washington is 212. The woman therefore often got calls that were meant for the then president, Lyndon B. Johnson.

She received a letter from the President saying that he could not be more grateful for the diplomatic way she handled the White House calls. In receiving the calls, Mrs Brown of Glendale, Queens, had always been polite to the sometimes distinguished callers.

Mr President promised that he would try to be just as polite in his reception of calls that were meant for Mrs Brown and her family.

A Nice Long Bath

A young Edinburgh housewife was on holiday for a week and one morning after her husband had gone to work, she decided to take a nice long bath. She put some of her favourite magazines and books on a chair alongside, turned the tap on and poured in some of her favourite bath salts. She went into her bedroom and undressed and walked naked to the bathroom, forgetting to take a towel from the airing cupboard in the hall.

She was just about to step into the bath when the telephone rang so she went to answer it. She grabbed the door handle, and to her horror the doorknob came off in her hand. Worse, the bar that worked the latch on the other side slipped out and fell on the hall floor. There she was, marooned in the bathroom with no clothes, not even a towel to wrap around herself. All she could do was jump into the bathtub; and whenever the water became too cold, she topped it up with hot water.

Her nice long bath lasted eight and half hours until her husband came home from work.

★　　★　　★　　★

.............As the industrial lift in which he was working crashed sixty feet towards the ground, a Liverpool glazier waited until the very last second before he jumped out, escaping with a slightly twisted ankle. The other four men in the lift were all seriously injured........................

★　　★　　★　　★

A Matchless Achievement

A German man's hobby was making models out of matchsticks. He entered a competition held each year in Cologne, but his efforts were never deemed worthy of a prize, so for two years he burned the midnight oil and produced a stunning matchstick model of Cologne Cathedral – perfect in every detail.

The night before the contest he decided to stay up all night and guard his model in case anyone tried to steal it. He made himself comfortable, lit his pipe – and unfortunately fell asleep. His pipe fell into the model and set fire to it, destroying it completely, as well as half of his house. He has now given up smoking – and model making.

Where's He Gone?

The dramatic critic of a well-known London newspaper was walking along a small street in Torremolinos with a friend. Neither had been there before and as they walked they pointed things out to each other and chattered happily, neither paying much attention to what the other said.

At one stage the friend turned round to say something to the critic and was astonished to find that he had vanished.

Assuming that his companion had turned into a side street to explore something of interest, the friend returned to their hotel, expecting the critic to turn up in time for dinner.

Four hours later, long after the meal had been consumed and when the friend was beginning to think about contacting the police, the critic turned up at the hotel, his head swathed in bandages.

It turned out that he had been so busy looking at the sights, he had not noticed that a manhole cover had been removed from the pavement and had simply fallen down it while his friend carried on talking, completely unaware of what had happened.

A Very Narrow Escape

In March, 1958, a B-47 plane took off from Hunter Air Base in Savannah, Georgia, on a routine flight to North Africa. At 14,000 feet the plane was over the small town of Florence, South Carolina travelling at 450 knots.

Suddenly a bright red light on the console told the pilot that the cargo that was being carried in an undercarriage, was rocking rather violently. A few seconds later the electric locks failed and the shackle opened allowing the cargo to fall out and smash down to the ground below. It struck the earth a few yards away from the home of one of the residents of Florence. He was awarded $50,000 compensation after a long court battle.

What was the cargo? A live atomic bomb. When it crashed to the ground, the triggering mechanism went off with a force of several hundred pounds of TNT. The blast tore up trees, wrecked Mr Gregg's house and damaged a church half a mile away. Fortunately the nuclear warhead didn't go off, but there was a crater 35 feet deep and 75 feet wide in the garden.

Wholly Matrimony

.................Being matters of a marital nature.........

It's A Man's Life

George I of Great Britain never brought his wife from Germany when he inherited the throne. Because of her adultery, he had her imprisoned for 32 years at Ahlden Castle in his native Hanover. He, however, arrived to take up his throne accompanied by his two mistresses.

Peter the Great of Russia was equally unforgiving of his wife's unfaithfulness. When he discovered her guilty secret, he had her lover executed and decapitated. The head was then preserved in an alcohol-filled jar and placed in the unfortunate queen's bedroom as a lesson to her.

Nisi, Nisi

On 17 July, 1975, a London High Court judge granted a decree nisi against a Muslim security officer who worked in Walworth. Fifteen minutes later he granted a decree nisi against the same man. Under Muslim law, a man is entitled to have four wives.

The Meat Was Undercooked, M'lud

A 54-year-old Frenchman, believed that cooking was the most important duty for any housewife. In 1956 his first wife served him an undercooked roast. A row followed that went on until the couple went to bed. He continued the argument and eventually became so angry that he threw her out of bed so violently that she broke her neck and died. He was jailed for seven years after which time he was released for good conduct.

Ten years later he was in court again. He had remarried on coming out of prison. One night a row broke out over a religious television programme. The Frenchman was so incensed by the programme that he fell into a foul mood. Later on in the evening, his wife presented him with an overcooked roast for supper. He was so angry that he struck her. She fell and broke her neck and died. He was sentenced to eight years' imprisonment.

I Do. But Why? Because I Love Him

The row that Eleanore Giacolone had with her boyfriend Johnny Campagna would have finished most romances. In a fit of rage one night he bashed her with a pole, then assaulted her with an ice-scraper and then stabbed her with a pitchfork. She was rushed to hospital and treated for broken ribs and a damaged spleen. She was lucky to be alive at all, the medics in the hospital thought when she left hospital a few weeks later. Two weeks after that she smiled serenely as she repeated her wedding vows in front of the minister who married her to Johnny.

'Why did I marry him?' she said afterwards. 'I love him. He's very like me in a lot of ways and I'm crazy about him.'

★ ★ ★ ★

. . . . *The women of Ancient Greece used to count their ages from the day they were married rather than the day they were born. It was considered that life only began for women after they were married.* . . . .

★ ★ ★ ★

Don't Be Late, Wife

Mr Parkinson of Los Angeles owned a news stand quite close to his house. From there he could see his wife leave to do the shopping and come back in with her groceries. He allowed her exactly one hour a day to do this. If she was as much as five minutes late he would beat her black and blue. He was so obsessed with the idea that some other man would try to steal his wife that, apart from her one hour's shopping, he refused to let her go out, unless he accompanied her.

On one occasion he saw a delivery man leave the house and, so convinced was he that he'd been up to no good with his wife, he asked a passer-by to watch the stand for a few minutes, ran back to the house and ripped up every flower in the garden and chopped down a tree that his wife had grown from a sapling. This was the last straw for Mrs Parkinson. She packed her bags and left him. How long had her husband been behaving like this? THIRTY YEARS.

It Always Ends In Tears

The scene: a unisex hairdressing salon in San Francisco. The characters: James and Dorothy, two customers, and Archibald, Dorothy's husband.

James was very attracted to Dorothy and when he struck up a conversation with her, she responded happily. She was, Dorothy told James, a model in Hollywood and her husband was an executive in a large public relations company, also in Hollywood. James told Dorothy, in a smooth upper class accent that he was divorced and owned a prosperous manufacturing company. Both believed each other implicitly.

In fact James came from a humble family and worked as a bicycle salesman; true, he was divorced. He had once had dreams of becoming a Hollywood movie star, and the more Dorothy talked about her connections there, the more his old dreams came back to him. Here was his passport to fame and riches, provided he could charm her enough. He did not have to try very hard, for Dorothy had never modelled in her life and her husband was the owner and operator of a concrete mixer. As she listened to James's smooth line of talk she found herself thinking that here was her chance to move into a better class of society. Here was a man who could satisfy her craving for fashionable clothes and expensive jewels.

The two, I suppose inevitably, became lovers but before they found out the truth about each other, Dorothy's husband became suspicious of Dorothy continually coming home late every night, and one day followed her to James's one-storey house on the outskirts of San Francisco. His suspicions confirmed, he decided to take his revenge, and when James came home two nights later he found his bedroom window open. What he discovered inside filled him with horror, for Archibald had backed his cement mixer up to James's window, forced it open and emptied two tons of concrete into the room, leaving a solidly set floor, four feet thick from wall to wall.

Archibald was given a six-month suspended sentence, ordered to pay $15,000 in costs and damages and is suing Dorothy for divorce. James and Dorothy don't see each other any more, not even at the hairdresser's.

★   ★   ★   ★

. . . . *An English High Court judge ruled that a woman found guilty of unlawfully killing her husband with a kitchen knife was not eligible for a widow's pension because she had, he said, brought her widowhood on herself.* . . . .

★   ★   ★   ★

Here's My Address, What's Yours?

A New York girl decided to go down to Miami for a holiday. While she was there she met and fell in love with a handsome man, also on holiday. As the vacation progressed, so too did the romance and near the end, the man asked the girl to marry him. The delighted girl said 'Yes', amazed that a simple holiday should turn out to be a whirlwind romance. The two exchanged addresses and found out that they both lived in the same apartment building in Brooklyn, New York.

A Strange Beginning To A Courtship

Bill Fralick was grateful to find a job as maintenance man at a hotel in Laconia, New Hampshire. After a few days he was called to check out a problem in the ladies room. He thought it was a blocked sink, but when he investigated, all the sinks were in perfect working order.

Then he heard a woman's voice shout, 'I can't get out, I'm stuck.'

Bill got to work with his screwdriver, slipped the lock mechanism and turned it from the outside. On the other side of the door, looking very embarrassed, was the Head Housekeeper. Without exchanging a word, the two left the ladies room.

A couple of days later they passed each other in the corridor and smiled at each other – still very embarrassed by what had happened.

However, seven months later they thought they had got over their embarrassment and they were married. But the first thing they did when they moved into their house was take the lock off the bathroom door.

I Do Because I Suppose I Have To

A Birmingham salesman was invited to a wedding at Avon. The invitation said that his best friend was being married. He duly turned up in church and was met by his girlfriend who smilingly handed him a wedding ring.

'You'll be needing this,' she said sweetly and before he had time to argue, the 'wedding guest' found himself exchanging vows and being married to Rosemary.

He said later that his new wife and he had been living together for more than two years and he had often asked her to marry him, but she had always refused.

The proud bride said, 'I thought it would be jolly good sport to surprise him.'

Age Is No Barrier

Curtis Petty Jr grew up two houses away from Mary Hillman in Flat Rock, Michigan. He often did chores for her – he mowed her lawn and ran errands for her. Eventually the couple decided to get married, much to the fury of Mary's children – and her grandchildren! In fact Curtis was younger than Mary's grandchildren. He was 24 when they got married – his bride was 83.

★   ★   ★   ★

.............*A High Court judge granted a divorce on the grounds that the plaintiff's wife had acted unreasonably in insisting that, when he came home, he kiss first her, then her sister – and then the cat.* ....

★   ★   ★   ★

Will You Marry Me – Ouch

The thirteenth-century Tartar princess, Aiyavuk, used to challenge all men who wanted to marry her to wrestle with her. She would agree only to marry the man who could beat her. If the man lost, he had to forfeit 100 horses to the princess. By the time she was eventually beaten, she had acquired 10,000 horses.

Don't Throw Rice At This Wedding

Every day for twenty-two years a Turkish wife served her husband rice twice a day for lunch and supper. She died and the not-too-upset widower met and fell in love with another woman. They have since got married, but before they did he made it a condition that not so much as a grain of rice should ever come into his house again.

I Don't Like My Son-In-Law

A certain English woman did not approve of her son-in-law. He was constantly hard up and her daughter was forced to scrimp and save in order to run the house. The woman offered her daughter £25 if she would leave her husband, and the girl took it, packed her bags and went home to Mummy. At least that's what the heartbroken husband is claiming in court where he is suing the woman for breaking up his marriage.

A Record Divorce

A 32-year-old German woman obtained a divorce from her husband in a Munster court on the grounds that her husband cared more about his collection of records than he did about her. On the day he came home with his 6,000th disc, she decided that that was enough and packed her bags.

She told the judge that the money she gave him to buy clothes for their daughter, Kerstin, was spent on records and he played Rolling Stones records at most inappropriate moments in their married life.

The judge ordered the man to pay £96 a month maintenance to his wife and daughter.

Hearing this, the man muttered 'I could have bought 20 new albums for that.'

His ex-wife has now married another man who doesn't own a record player.

A Kitchen Sink Drama

A Jugoslavian plumber was called out one morning to attend to a blocked sink in the house of a newly married couple. The wife was out when he arrived at the house and when she returned she saw a pair of legs sticking out from under the sink. She thought that they belonged to her husband and being very newly wed did something rather intimate.

The astonished plumber jumped up and banged his head on the sink, knocking himself out. The panic-stricken girl called an ambulance and by the time it came the plumber had recovered consciousness. He was placed on a stretcher and while he was being carried down the stairs one of the stretcher-bearers asked what had happened.

He thought it was so funny that he dropped the stretcher and the unfortunate plumber tumbled down the stairs and broke a leg. The woman's husband was also slightly disturbed – his wife was so upset by what had happened that she withdrew from the marital bed for quite some time, saying that the incident had completely put her off sex.

Limelight Cordial

.... *Being matters of a kind*
concerning famous people.............................

An Ill-Fitted Match

Before she met and married Prince Rainier of Monaco, the late Princess Grace was the well-known film star, Grace Kelly. Throughout the 1950s she was one of the most popular of all Hollywood actresses. Her name was linked romantically with Clark Gable, perhaps the most famous of all post-war Hollywood heartthrobs. It is said that they were on the point of marriage (before Ms Kelly had met her prince) but there was one thing about Mr Gable that she found immensely irritating. He wore a very ill-fitting set of dentures which clicked together whenever he talked.

Lucas — Aid

George Lucas was a young Hollywood film director who had a great idea for a movie. He budgeted it and decided that it could be filmed and edited for around $700,000. He found a backer in United Artists, but they withdrew at the last minute. Eventually, after a great deal of dithering, Universal Pictures backed the movie which went on to be one of their most successful films of the 1970s – *American Graffiti*.

Having finished the movie, Mr Lucas then came up with another idea which he thought was a winner. But even Universal, who had made a lot of money out of *American Graffiti*, turned it down. Eventually Twentieth Century Fox gave him some backing. The men at Universal must still be kicking themselves, for the film eventually grossed more than $300 million even without television and video rights. The film? STAR WARS.

A Painful Experience

John Dillinger, the notorious prohibition gangster, decided to change his fingerprints as a way of evading prosecution. He dipped his fingers into a bowl of acid and went through weeks of agony while his burnt fingers healed. He was more than slightly distressed to find that his 'new' fingerprints were exactly the same as the original ones.

Fair Exchange?

It is the custom when the British Royal Family make State visits overseas or receive foreign Heads of State in Great Britain, that gifts are exchanged. When the Queen and the Duke of Edinburgh visited the Middle East in 1980 they received some beautiful jewellery.

But perhaps the oddest exchange occurred when the British Royal Family gave President Geisel of Brazil and his wife a set of Charles Bentley sketches, a 1648 edition of the *Natural History of Brazil*, a gold and enamel brooch and a carriage clock. In exchange they were presented with six toucans, two giant ant-eaters, a sloth, an armadillo and two black-necked swans.

Sit Up Straight – Forever

Poet Ben Jonson was honoured with a place in Poet's Corner in Westminster Abbey when he died in 1637. Unfortunately the space allocated to him was too small to allow him to be buried in the traditional way – so he was buried in a sitting position.

No Smoking

Annie Oakley, of *Annie Get Your Gun* fame, was one of the most famous marksmen – sorry markswomen – of her day. The crown prince of Germany, Prince William, once allowed her to shoot the ash from a cigarette that he was holding between his lips – from one hundred feet away.

★　　★　　★　　★

. . . . His Grace, the Archbishop of Canterbury, when he was Bishop of St Albans, used to dread wearing his purple robes in the street in case, if he was knocked down, he should be taken for a transvestite. . . . .

★　　★　　★　　★

Curtains For The Lady Of Lyons

Lord Lytton, an eminent Victorian literary figure, was very proud of a play he had written called *The Lady of Lyons*. He was convinced that it would run for a respectable length of time. The first night audience was full of literary and society people. After waiting for one hour they all left the theatre as no one could raise the safety curtain. The play never opened.

But Was It Worth The Money?

James VI of Scotland became King of England on the death of his mother's cousin, Queen Elizabeth. Like many kings, he had his favourites and took them with him when he went to London. Many of his subjects were furious at the privileges that he granted them; feeling was especially strong against the Earl of Stirling who was granted the lands of CANADA for an annual rent of ONE PENNY PER ANNUM.

The First US President Served In The British Army

George Washington served for nearly six years in the British Army and rose to the rank of colonel. It was during these years that he became a skilled leader of men, a talent he used to full effect when he led the American Army against the British during the War of Independence.

Rain Stops Play (Almost)

At the Royal Opera House, Covent Garden one night in October 1982 during a performance of Mussorgsky's opera *Khovanshchina*, raindrops were seen falling on the chorus on stage. It seems that the roof, which had recently been repaired, was leaking. The chorus bravely carried on singing.

Coincidentally, thousands of miles away at about the same time, the Queen was visiting the island of Kiribita in the South Seas. For days before her visit the rain had poured down in torrents. In order to ensure that it cleared up for Her Majesty's arrival, the authorities called for a local magician, Iosiabate, to stop the rain. In great secrecy the magician worked his spells and then, by custom, disappeared to make them work. Ten minutes before the Queen stepped ashore, the rain stopped.

Third Time Unlucky

Oliver Cromwell won two of his greatest victories on the third of September, one at Dunbar and one at Worcester. If he began to think of it as his lucky day he was wrong. For he died on the third of September in 1658.

★   ★   ★   ★

. . . . *Lord Nelson chose to be buried in St Paul's Church in London rather than in Westminster Abbey because he believed that Westminster was sinking into the nearby River Thames.* . . . .

77

At The Count Of Five

Former Prime Minister James Callaghan was usually very kind to press photographers who wanted to snap him. He did not mind stopping for a few extra moments to make sure that the paperazzi had good shots of him.

During a visit to the new Anglo-Australian premises in London in 1978 he was asked to unveil a wooden plaque to commemorate the event. He told the press that he would count to five and then pull the ribbon.

The cameras focused on him and the Prime Minister duly counted one ... two ... three ... four ... five.

When he said 'five' all the flashlights went off and the cameras got a perfect picture of Mr Callaghan pulling the plaque right off the wall.

Shoo, Your Majesty

During a visit to Toronto, the Queen was invited to a horse-shoeing competition. The competitors were instructed that under no circumstances were the horses' rears to be allowed to face Her Majesty, 'for reasons of protocol'. The Queen took great interest in one of the competitors, but her interest was disastrous for the 'smith. As Her Majesty walked around the horse the 'smith was forced to hop around away from her in order to keep to his instructions.

A Deadly Obsession

Sarah Bernhardt, the famous French actress was obsessed with death.

When she was a teenager in Paris one of her favourite occupations was to visit the city morgue and look at the unclaimed corpses of derelicts who had been dragged from the River Seine.

Before she was twenty, she persuaded her mother to buy her a rosewood coffin lined with white satin. She often slept in it and was buried in it when she died aged seventy-nine.

Sorry, Ma'am

Lady Diana Cooper was, and still is, one of the greatest society beauties of the twentieth century. Unfortunately, her sight has failed slightly with the advancing years, and without her glasses she is very short-sighted.

At a concert to celebrate the hundredth birthday of Sir Robert Mayer, Lady Diana found herself talking to a chatty little woman who came up to her and seemed to know her quite well. It was only after a few minutes that Lady Diana realized to whom she was chatting.

'I am sorry, ma'am,' she blurted out, 'I didn't recognize you without your crown,' and desperately tried to bob a curtsy to Her Majesty the Queen.

A Common Investiture

In 1843 William Wordsworth was appointed Poet Laureate. For the ceremony at Buckingham Palace he had to borrow a suit from fellow poet Samuel Rogers. Seven years later, his successor Alfred, Lord Tennyson went to the Palace to be formally appointed to the same honour. He borrowed the same suit from the same poet. Poor Mr Rogers' suit seems to have lasted longer than his poetry.

The Spirit Of The Lord

At the end of the Battle of Culloden in 1746, the devoutly Roman Catholic Lord Strathallan lay mortally wounded on the battlefield. There was no bread or water available for the priest who was attending to administer the Holy Eucharist – so oatcakes were used in place of bread – washed down with malt whisky.

★   ★   ★   ★

. . . . Gustav III of Sweden was so convinced that coffee was poisonous that he ordered a convicted murderer to be executed by drinking cup after cup of it. He didn't die. .

A Floating Experience

Dame Janet Baker is still one of the greatest female singers of today. Although she has retired from the opera stage, she performs frequently at concerts.

Shortly after her retirement from opera, she was singing in Berlioz's *Damnation of Faust* at the Festival Hall in London. The previous evening there had been a Hallowe'en concert during which members of the audience had floated helium-filled balloons around the hall.

Unfortunately, during Dame Janet's performance some of the balloons which had not been removed floated against the lights and exploded with loud bangs. The laughing audience then watched as two of the balloons floated harmlessly down to the auditorium - one fell among the audience and the other into the orchestra. Dame Janet, being a true professional, carried on singing as though nothing had happened.

It Wasn't Cheating – Exactly

Mary Pickford was only five feet high and became the most famous star of her day. Many of the roles that she played were children and the sets of her films were specially built to make her look smaller than she really was. All the furniture and props were made one-third larger than usual, windows and doors were bigger than normal, and doorknobs were placed slightly higher to make it look as if she had to stretch to get up to them.

Reheaded

The Duke of Monmouth was executed in 1685 for his part in the unsuccessful plot to overthrow his uncle, King James II.

It was only after he had been beheaded that it was decided to paint an official portrait of him. His head was skilfully (if ghoulishly) stitched back on to his body. The corpse was then dressed in his own original suit of clothes and posed carefully for the artist.

WE APOLOGISE FOR THE LATE ARRIVAL OF THE 11.35 UNIFORM ON PLATFORM 3 ...

And The Band Played

The royal train carrying King Edward VII of Great Britain, drew into the station at Rathenau in Germany on February 9, 1909, during the King's state visit. The welcoming military band struck up God Save the King and the reception committee shuffled nervously, expecting the King to step down from the train before the National Anthem was finished. The band played it once through, but there was no sign of the King ... so they played it again, but still the King did not appear. The conductor raised his baton and the Anthem was played for a third time ... and a fourth ... and a fifth ...

Sixteen play-throughs later, the King eventually appeared at the door of the carriage, resplendent in the uniform of Field Marshal of the Imperial German Army. The reason for the delay was that the uniform was so tight the portly King had been struggling to get into it all the time the band had been playing on the platform.

★ ★ ★ ★

. . . . .Albert Einstein, one of the most formidably clever men of this century, failed the entrance exam for Zurich Polytechnic when he was sixteen. . . . .

Professional Jealousy?

Ernest Hemingway was a keen amateur boxer and when in Paris often worked out with a fellow American called Morley Callaghan.

One day when the two were getting ready to box at the American Club, fellow writer Scott Fitzgerald stopped by and Hemingway asked him to keep time.

The first round began and Hemingway and Callaghan were evenly matched. After three minutes, Fitzgerald called time and allowed the usual minute's rest before beginning the second

round. The fight began to go in Callaghan's favour, and he drew some blood from the American writer. This infuriated Hemingway who began desperately to counter-attack, but Callaghan was more than a match for him.

Fitzgerald was so spellbound by the fight that he forgot all about the stop-watch in his hand, until after about four minutes Hemingway was knocked to the ground. He yelled out that he had let the round go on far too long and Hemingway, picking himself up, shouted, 'All right, Scott. If you want to see me get the hell knocked out of me just say so. Only don't say that you made a mistake.'

Prince Uncharming

The young man walking along one of Monte Carlo's exclusive beaches recognized the beautiful television and film star relaxing on her own in the Mediterranean sun. He had read that her romance with one of Hollywood's most famous Romeos was in shreds and thought that he might be able to ingratiate himself into her company.

He sat down and had a waiter page him – Prince Urbano Barberini. The actress was impressed when she saw the handsome prince answer the paging call and the two struck up an instant friendship.

She was bowled over by his charming manners and the friends whose names he dropped into the conversation – including the daughters of the local royal family. For three days the two were inseparable, lunching and dining together.

They even flew to Paris, the actress picking up the bills all the way. It was only there that she discovered that her prince was, in fact, a nineteen-year-old ne'er-do-well with not an ounce of royal blood in his veins. She prefers not to talk about the incident today.

★　　★　　★　　★

. . . . In 1857 the French poet Baudelaire was fined for publishing six obscene poems in **Les Fleurs du Mal.** *He was later pardoned – in 1949, 82 years after his death. . . . . . .*

★　　★　　★　　★

Not Again, Crew

The crewmen of the *Bounty* were not the only ones who mutinied against the infamous Captain Bligh. When he later became Governor of Australia, he did his best to eliminate rum smuggling. A rebellion resulted from his high-handed attitude and the officers of the New South Wales Corps arrested Bligh and held him prisoner until a replacement governor arrived in Australia the following year.

A Sentimental Phonebox

A very famous Welsh pop-singer who now lives and works mainly in the United States grew up in comparative poverty in a small Welsh town where very few people had the telephone installed in their houses. When he wanted to call his girlfriend, now his wife, he had to use a callbox on the corner, and very often the couple used the box to carry on their romance if there was nowhere else to go.

When he bought a huge mansion in Bel-Air, California he contacted the council of his home town, bought the telephone box from them and had it flown over to America and installed in his $4,000,000 residence.

A Really Quick Worker

Enid Blyton was one of the most popular children's authors of her generation. Her books still sell in vast quantities, more than fifteen years after her death. She wrote more than 600 books in her lifetime and was an amazingly quick worker.

But her agent did not realize just how quick until one Friday afternoon when he telephoned her and asked if he could come down and see her that evening to discuss some business. She said that it would not be convenient as she was planning to start one of her well-known Famous Five books that day and she planned her whole weekend around her work schedule; why didn't he, she said, come down the following Thursday for lunch? He agreed to do so and turned up on the appointed day.

'I'm so glad you came today,' she said when he arrived. 'We can kill two birds with one stone.'

At which she gave him her new manuscript, which she had not started until after she had talked to him the previous Friday. It was a 50,000 word manuscript which was duly submitted to her publisher who produced it without changing so much as one comma.

★   ★   ★   ★

. . . . .Henry VIII loved gambling but was often short of money to pay his gambling debts. He once lost the bells of Saint Paul's Church. . . . .

85

Odd Bods

.................*Being matters of a medical or physical nature*...

Nor Yet A Drop To Drink

A 35-year-old Somerset man has, as part of a strange diet, to eat lots and lots of juice-bearing fruits and vegetables, such as apples, oranges and tomatoes. Nothing odd about that you may say; after all, many diets specify large intakes of fruit.

But the reason for this one is that the unfortunate man is allergic to all liquids – including water. He last drank a glass in 1980 and it made him terribly ill.

Some friends gave him a bottle of special mineral water. He took a sip which immediately gave him a dreadful headache and affected his legs so badly that he could not walk for the rest of the day.

So he's sticking to his odd diet until doctors work out a cure for him.

It's A Boy...

Little Gregory was a healthy baby boy. EVERYTHING about him was perfectly normal. When he was thirteen months old, he had to be taken into hospital for a hernia operation. Doctors discovered that a vital piece of the little boy's identity was in fact an enlarged piece of a little girl's identity and Gregory was actually a girl. He ... sorry she, is now called Marjorie.

All Join In The Last Verse

When a missionary called Herr Schwartz died in Delhi at the end of the nineteenth century, a large crowd turned up for his funeral, so highly regarded was he.

Herr Schwartz had specified in his will that his favourite hymn was to close the ceremony. His wishes were duly respected and the congregation, many of them openly moved, began to sing the hymn.

When they reached the last verse, they were thunderstruck to hear Herr Schwartz's voice coming from the coffin, joining in the singing. He had been incorrectly certified as dead, and came to just in time.

Something Nasty Under The Sink

Before moving to Atlanta, Georgia, a certain Mr Rodrique used to rent an apartment in Hamden, Connecticut. He occasionally took his work home as he found he did not have enough time where he worked to do everything that he wanted to. When he moved he unfortunately left some of the work behind and the new tenants were horrified when they looked under the sink and found a pair of nicely dissected human arms there. Mr Rodrique is an orthopaedic surgeon and had taken the arms home from Yale School of Medicine because he was not getting enough laboratory time for study. In the haste of packing up and moving he had simply forgotten that the arms were there.

★   ★   ★   ★

. . . . .The funny bone is not a bone, but the ulnar nerve which runs in a shallow groove close to the skin on the inside of the elbow. . . . .

★   ★   ★   ★

Don't Be Shy

The nurse in the emergency ward in an Edinburgh hospital was quite used to men being shy when she had to ask them to remove their trousers, but the burly young man who had come in with a badly cut leg was extremely reluctant to do so.

'Come on,' she said, 'I'm a trained nurse and am quite used to this you know.'

'Very well,' said the man eventually, 'but please don't get the wrong impression.'

The nurse watched as the embarrassed man removed his pants to reveal that he was wearing a black suspender belt, holding up dark stockings. He had been dressing to go to a fancy dress party with his wife. He had intended to go as a nurse and had put on the unusual undergarments.

While putting on the dress he had tripped and fallen, cutting his leg very badly. He pulled on a pair of trousers and a sweater and his wife had driven him to hospital forgetting that he was wearing her underwear.

I THINK HE'S GONE OVER THE TOP WITH THAT EYEPATCH AND TELESCOPE!

A Leg Bye

At Greenwich Hospital, a home for retired sailors, two teams organized a cricket match. At the end of the day, the winners had won by 103 runs. Nothing unusual about that, you might say. Well, the losers had all lost an arm – and the winners were all one-legged.

Stand By Your Desks

Two of America's top business executives, the Chairman of Kelloggs and the President of IBM, as well as the Vice-Chairman of the Federal Reserve Board, all had something in common apart from being successful. They all suffered from bad backs, brought about, their osteopaths said, by spending too long each day sitting at their desks.

So, too, did the Chairman of Prudential Insurance Co. of America. He realized that although his dentist stood all day he never suffered from a bad back, so he had a special desk designed for himself that allowed him to work and stand at the same time. It worked so well that the other top executives mentioned did the same.

All now heartily recommend standing desks not just for those with bad backs, but for anyone who does not want to feel physically exhausted at the end of the day.

Thanks To The Cigarettes

The voice of the phenomenally successful *ET* (extra-terrestrial), Steven Spielberg's record-breaking money-spinning film, was something of a problem. Technicians could not come up with a voice to match the appearance of the model star of the film. By pure chance, Mr Spielberg happened to be in a store one day when he heard a lady ordering something. Her voice, he thought, was exactly what he wanted, and so unknown American housewife Pat Welsh's voice became part of the biggest money-making movie of all time. Mrs Welsh used to be a speech trainer – but excessive cigarette smoking caused her voice to crack up, leaving her croaky and gasping for breath – exactly what Mr Spielberg had in mind.

May I Borrow Your Breast, Madam?

A Zimbabwe businessman was attempting to remove a dangerous cobra which had slithered into the engine of his car, when the snake spat at him and with deadly accuracy landed her stinging venom right in his eye. This usually causes blindness.

Fortunately, a lorry driver who had parked nearby saw what had happened and pulled the agonized man into the cabin of his truck, where his wife was breast-feeding her baby. He pushed him over to the astonished woman and told her to squirt some milk into his eyes. This diluted the venom and the 'victim's' eyesight was saved.

Oh Brother

A Moscow woman has given birth to ... wait for it ... sixteen sets of twins. That makes 32 children. As well as seven sets of triplets (another 21) and four sets of quads (another 16). That makes 69 children altogether.

An Odd Mouthful

There are many instances of seeds becoming lodged between the teeth of people whose oral hygiene could be better, and which take root and sprout. But there is only one recorded instance of an unfortunate woman whose fillings are so arranged that when the atmospheric conditions are right, they pick up commercial radio signals, particularly long-wave ones.

A Near Miss

Peter Lenz, a twenty-year-old West German, received his call-up papers one day. He did not relish having to spend two years in the West German Army and he knew that he could only be excused on medical grounds. Fortunately, his girlfriend was diabetic so when he went to the Medical Officer to be examined, he took with him a specimen of her urine. When he was asked to supply a sample, he switched his girlfriend's urine for his own.

He went home confident that he would be told not to report back. He was astonished therefore a few days later to receive a letter telling him that he had been passed fit and to report to his unit.

When he did so, the recruiting officer told him, 'We would have believed that you were diabetic, but not that you're pregnant, too.'

★　　★　　★　　★

.............*In 1941 Elaine Esposito of Florida, USA, unfortunately lapsed into a coma. She died without regaining consciousness – 37 years later in 1978...................*

★　　★　　★　　★

No Conception

The natives of a part of northern India listened intently as a member of the World Health Organization talked to them about contraception. To demonstrate the use of a condom sheath, the doctor rolled one over a convenient piece of wood. The natives nodded in understanding and the doctor left, convinced that the birth rate in the area, which had been dangerously high, would begin to fall. A few years later he revisited the place and was surprised to see more children than ever before. 'But haven't you been using contraceptives?', he asked the people.

'Yes,' they replied. 'We did as you said but they don't work.'

He asked them to demonstrate how they were being used, and, sure enough, one of the men produced a sheath and ceremoniously rolled it over a convenient piece of wood.

I'll Get You In The End

John Hunter was an eighteenth century surgeon who was keen to dissect the body of a local giant, Charles Byrne, who because of a tumour in his pituitary gland had grown to a height of more than seven feet. Byrne did not like the idea of having his body cut up after death so he refused his permission. Undaunted, Hunter simply hired a private detective to follow Byrne everywhere.

He eventually died of tuberculosis in 1783 and the undertaker was bribed to take the body to Hunter's hospital.

For Love Of A Cuppa

The tea in the hospital where a woman lay waiting for an operation was not to her liking. So, before she was due to be operated on, she got out of bed, went home, made herself a decent cuppa and returned to hospital – all in her dressing gown.

★   ★   ★   ★

. . . . *The normal human body temperature is 98.4°F. The highest temperature where the patient survived is 112°F.* . . . .

A Varied Diet (Or An Iron Tonic)

In 1960, the Journal of the American Medical Association reported that a patient checked into a hospital to have treatment for a swollen ankle. X-rays revealed that he had swallowed 26 keys, 39 nail files, 88 coins – as well as a three-pound piece of metal.

That's Her Foot

An old lady died after a long illness that necessitated having her foot amputated, in a hospital in Florida. Her body was put into the morgue locker with a plastic bag containing her personal belongings and another containing her foot. A funeral undertaker collected the body and the two bags, not realizing that one of them contained the foot. He took the parcels round to Ada's relatives where her son-in-law reached into the unmarked parcel and withdrew the amputated foot, to his own horror and the screams of his wife and sister-in-law. Embarrassed hospital officials have agreed in an out-of-court settlement to pay more than $10,000 compensation.

Eye, Eye

The eyes are the most sensitive of all the body's organs. It has been estimated that they are capable of differentiating 10 million different shades. The average eye can see an object 4/1000th of an inch long from ten inches away, and some people with extraordinarily good vision can see light shining through a hole 1/6000th of an inch across. People with such excellent sight can recognize human faces from one mile away. Wonderful if you want to avoid someone coming towards you.

★　　★　　★　　★

. . . . When Berkshire mothers-to-be received forms asking if they wanted polio injections, they were amused to see that as well as their age, name and address, they were asked to fill in a box indicating their sex. . . . .

94

. . . .*An American strong man, has such powerful stomach muscles that when he once had a 104 pound cannon ball fired at him from close range on stage, it did him no harm whatsoever.* . . . .

The Ear Fairy

A Northamptonshire woman, who lived in Higham Ferrers, was quite hard of hearing, so in 1979 she went to her doctor and asked to have her ears syringed. The obliging doctor was astonished when he pulled out a baby tooth. It had been there for thirty years. When Janet was five she had lost the tooth and, following the time honoured custom, had put it under her pillow hoping that the tooth fairy would leave the usual sixpence (2.5np). After she fell asleep, the tooth had lodged in her ear, and stayed there for the next thirty years causing her no pain whatsoever.

95

Animal Crackers

.... Being matters of a kind concerning animals...

The Call Of The Wild

Noel Macabe of Derbyshire was relaxing one day in his home, listening to a record called *Cry of the Wild Geese*. There was a sudden breaking of glass as a Canadian Goose, eager to find its hidden noisy brothers, crashed through his window. Another two were apparently so overcome that they fell into the garden.

Only The Queen

The queen termite which is about 100 times larger than the other termites and which can lay about 1,000 eggs daily, secretes an acid that makes the other females sterile. If the queen becomes sterile, she is deprived of food and dies. Another female, deprived of the fluid, can then reproduce and become queen.

An Unwanted Passenger

A Midlands businessman was on a trip to Malaysia. He decided to take a few days off and see something of the country so he hired a small pick-up truck to drive from Singapore to Kota Bharu, a trip of around 350 miles.

At first everything went perfectly, but suddenly the weather changed and he found himself in the middle of a tropical storm. Driving became impossible so he pulled into the side of the road and waited until the rain had stopped before driving off again.

A few miles further on, changing gear he felt something warm and smooth move across his wrist. He looked down and saw a large python slithering through a gap in the floorboards. He slammed on the brakes, wanting to get out as fast as possible, but the snake was too quick for him and within seconds had wound itself round his body, squeezing the breath out of him.

The terrified businessman managed to grab the snake's head and tried to smash it against the car window. But the snake was too strong and the man thought he was going to die.

Suddenly he heard a screech of tyres and saw a lorry draw up alongside. The Malaysian driver jumped out and shouted at him to let it go.

The man did so and threw the snake's head away from him. Instantly the lorry driver cut its head off with his sharp knife. He then explained that the snake must have wound itself round the axle when the car had been parked and then got in through the floorboards. Apparently it happens quite often.

The lorry driver then asked if he could take the dead snake with him.

'Whatever for?' asked the businessman.

'Supper,' replied the lorry driver.

★　　★　　★　　★

.............It has been estimated that, between them, all the chickens in the world lay an awful lot of eggs every year – 400,000,000,000 to be precise. ....

Dinner Is Served — Woof Woof

The eighth Earl of Bridgewater used to give lavish dinner parties for his best friends. They were all dogs, and were dressed up in silk coats, satin breeches and leather shoes – the same clothes worn by aristocratic Englishmen of the day.

Hopped Off With My Wallet

An Australian farmer found a kangaroo caught in the wire fence around his property. The poor beast was shivering with fear as the kind-hearted farmer took off his waistcoat and slipped it onto the animal – impulsively fitting its paws through the armholes.

He set to work freeing the 'roo, which took about three hours. As soon as it was free, the animal hopped away, still wearing the farmer's waistcoat. He wasn't too upset as it was an old working 'coat anyway. But three hours later, while searching for his wallet, he remembered that it had been in the waistcoat pocket.

So, if you're ever in Australia and see a kangaroo hopping around wearing a waistcoat, try and catch it – it could be well worth your while.

Skunkorella, Or Is It Skunkorissima?

It is well known that the skunk emits a disgusting smell if it is frightened or in danger. At first it will growl and stamp the ground to warn its enemies. But if this is unheeded, the skunk turns its back, lifts its tail and squirts the secretion at its foe. The odour can be smelt half a mile away. The same secretion, with the foul odour removed, is used as a base for making expensive perfumes.

★　　★　　★　　★

. . . . .The rarest dog in the world is the Tahl-Tan bear dog. In 1982 there were only three of them living. . . . . . .

100

Trapped

The sixteenth century Dean of Hereford, a Dr Price, considered that he was socially superior to the other clergy and so decided that during a regular religious procession he would not walk with the others, but instead would ride on the back of a mare and read his prayer book as he went. Unfortunately a stallion broke loose and mounted the mare, leaving the embarrassed Dean completely trapped by 'horseplay'.

Not Biting Today, Boys

The anglers of the National Ambulance Service Championships held at Kidderminster in 1972 took up their places eager for a good day's fishing. There were two hundred of them altogether. Five hours later, when not one fish had been landed by any of the fishermen, they were told by a local passerby that they were wasting their time – all the fish had been moved to other waters three weeks earlier.

★   ★   ★   ★

. . . . In Buenos Aires, a cat called Mincha ran up a tree and stayed there for six years. Whilst up there, she gave birth to three lots of kittens. . . . .

★   ★   ★   ★

Dead Heat

Punters at a New South Wales racecourse cheered wildly as the three leading horses galloped towards the finishing line. None of the horses managed to put in that extra something necessary to win the race and the judges declared a triple dead heat. The race was re-run with only the three joint winners – High Flyer, Loch Lochie and Bardini – running. The expectant racegoers watched astonished as the three horses tied for first place again.

Better Than Paying Taxes

A tribe of Idaho Indians were given complete tax exemption when their lands were confiscated by the American government in the nineteenth century.

All they had to do was present the Governor of the state, once a year, with 20 beaver pelts in lieu of taxes. When beavers became more difficult to trap, this was amended to one deer and a turkey, which are still handed over to this day ...

I wonder if the Chancellor of the Exchequer would be interested in a frozen chicken or something similar.

I Don't Want To Know That

The South-east Asian cave swiftlet makes its nest from its saliva which hardens on the cave walls where the bird lives. It is these nests that are used to make bird's nest soup which is a great delicacy in some parts of the world.

FIRST TIME ANYBODY SENT THE BIRDS NEST SOUP BACK!

Come Home ... By Post

Pigeon racing is a popular sport all over the world. Owners take their birds to pre-arranged places, release them and the pigeons with unerring ability find their way home. In 1953, a keen pigeon fancier released his bird in Pembrokeshire expecting him to be home that evening. Eleven years later the bird turned up dead, in a box bearing a Brazilian postmark.

Snails Save Lives

To determine blood groups, there is a method of extracting a chemical from human blood which, when mixed with a sample of the blood in question will react in a particular way according to the blood group. However, to get enough of the solution a great deal of human blood is required. But fortunately, snails' eggs, which are the size of a pinhead, contain the same chemical – in fact, the blood of five donors would be required to supply the same amount of the chemical as is found in one of the snail's eggs.

He Dyed Hunting

An American millionaire on a deerstalking trip in Scotland decided that his white horse could be seen too easily by the deer. He bought two black dyes from a local hairdresser and set about changing the horse's colour with the aid of two brushes. The operation was successful. The black dye changed the horse's appearance completely. Unfortunately, the dye had such a powerful smell that the deer could smell it miles away, and the luckless millionaire returned empty-handed to America.

★ ★ ★ ★

.............*The coconut crab, a kind of hermit crab, climbs trees and picks coconuts.* ....

★ ★ ★ ★

An Inside Job

The hagfish has a unique way of killing its prey. This eel-like creature ties itself in a loop and attaches itself to a fish's gills by biting it with its sharp teeth. Twisting its knotted body around and around, the hagfish buries itself deeper and deeper into its victim until it is completely inside. Then it begins to eat its prey from the inside until only the skeleton and skin are left.

★　　★　　★　　★

.............The natives of Hawaii call one of the largest of their local fish by the simple name 'O'. By contrast, they call one of the smallest 'homomomonukunukuaguk'........

★　　★　　★　　★

Roommates Unwanted

Even the cleanest home contains approximately 452 species of assorted insects and vermin. But don't worry. A survey of a house in Kent carried out in 1860 revealed that there were 3,287 assorted 'animals' living there, including pinhole borers, cockroaches, booklice, bookworms, Pharaoh's ants, wasps, houseflies, bluebottles, greenfly, ladybirds, carpet beetles, moths, wood beetles, pipistrelles, bats, mice, rats, dormice, toads, millipedes, cellar beetles, mosquitoes, black beetles, black ants, flourworms, leather beetles, silverfish, steam flies, grain weevils, cheese mites, mealworms, earwigs, woodlice, slugs, earthworms, snails, spiders, firebrats, sparrows, house martins, centipedes ... and the human owners.

A Balanced Diet

When one of the ostriches in London Zoo died unexpectedly, the keepers decided to hold an autopsy. In its insides were found two handkerchiefs, three gloves, a film spool, part of a plastic comb, the winding key of an alarm clock, part of a rolled gold necklace, two collar studs and a Belgian franc piece.

Hard To Swallow

Vets have often been called out by distressed pet owners when the unfortunate animals have got something stuck in their throat. But Dr Deke Beusse was surprised when he was asked to remove a fish that got caught in the throat of a Tiger Shark.

High Freeze

One morning in 1974, an American housewife was astonished to see frozen ducks fall out of the sky in Arkansas. It turned out that a flock of ducks had flown so high that they had frozen to death in the air.

A B. . . . . . Painful Death

A recent Hollywood disaster movie about a killer swarm of bees is based on fact. A beekeeper in Sao Paolo, Brazil decided to cross gentle European bees with larger, more aggressive ones. His idea was to improve productivity, but unfortunately the vicious tendencies of the African bees were stronger than the European ones. Twenty-six swarms escaped and, led by their African Queens, began to attack animals and occasionally human beings, with fatal consequences.

Here, Boyo

£65 seemed reasonable for the trained sheepdog being advertised in a farming magazine. At least the Surrey farmer who stumped up thought so. Unfortunately for him the dog had been trained in Wales and could only respond to commands (other than whistles) in the Welsh language.

★　　★　　★　　★

. . . . *When cats hear a dog barking, the soles of their paws very often perspire.* . . . .

Breed Like Rabbits

Rabbits are the biggest animal pests in Australia. There are literally millions upon millions of them. They are all descended from six rabbits, three males and three females, who were let loose in the 1850s.

ER... I THINK I'LL ATTACK RUSSIA INSTEAD...

Not Tobite, Josephine

After the wedding celebrations were over and Napoleon had withdrawn to the bridal chamber with his bride, Josephine Beauharnais, her pet dog, mistaking the Little Corporal's amorous advances on his mistress as an assault, jumped on to the bed and bit him.

★　　★　　★　　★

. . . . *Sea hedgehogs, usually about a foot long, can kill sharks more than twenty feet long.* . . . .

Compassionate Leave Granted

Billy Smart, the late circus owner, had a grandson who became very fond of a whale that was part of the Smart menagerie. The young man was eventually called up to do his National Service. Unfortunately, the whale began to pine for him. Mr Smart contacted the authorities and requested that his grandson be given compassionate leave. The request was granted and the youth and the whale were happily reunited.

That's A Nice Insect You're Wearing

Women of Cuba have a most unusual way of making themselves attractive. They hang fireflies on their dresses and around their necks as decoration. Actually, the firefly is not a fly, it's a beetle. Inside its stomach there are five chemicals. When oxygen enters the firefly's body, it stimulates a nerve reaction which causes the chemicals to combine. This makes the firefly glow. A few seconds later another chemical combines with the other five and switches the fly off. Men travelling in tropical forests sometimes collect fireflies in jars and use them as emergency torches.

Roses For The Lady

Like most other ladies, a resident of Canterbury called Killa, enjoys being presented with a lovely bunch of roses now and again. But unlike most women, Killa eats them. She also has a taste for expensive chocolates and is always happy with a bunch of celery. Killa is a 60 pound female gorilla. One of her male companions in the zoo where she lives enjoys the odd gallon of beer.

★   ★   ★   ★

. . . .*In Kuala Lumpur an elephant once beat a team of 100 farmers at a tug o'war contest.* . . . .

Hundreds Of Thousands Of Ducks

Le Tour D'Argent is one of the smartest restaurants in Paris. Since it first opened in 1582 the rich and famous have flocked to it to sample the renowned cooking and superb wines. In 1890 Frederic Delair became Master Chef and began a tradition which is still in existence today. The speciality of the house is duck, and he decided that every duck that is served should be served with a card giving the bird's number.

In October 1982, the restaurant's 400th anniversary, the 600,000th duck was served.

★   ★   ★   ★

. . . . During the All-Ireland Frog Swallowing Championships, John Macnamara of County Clare was declared the winner after swallowing five live frogs in 65 seconds. . . . .

★   ★   ★   ★

He Had No Right To Be There

In 1872 the viceroy of India was on a hunting trip and one night when he went to bed he woke up when he felt something heavy on his body. He opened his eyes and saw a huge cobra coiled up on his chest.

He knew that if he moved the cobra would strike and kill him, so he lay dead still for almost an hour, when suddenly someone came into his tent. The man saw the snake and left the tent. A few minutes later he returned carrying a jugful of steaming hot milk. He put it down as close as he could to the cobra's head and within a few minutes the snake, sensing the warmth coming from the pot, uncoiled itself from the viceroy's chest and slithered into the jug. The man rammed the lid on and trapped the cobra.

The viceroy was astonished when his saviour asked him to say nothing about the escapade. It turned out that he was a wandering thief who had been looking for rich pickings from the viceroy's camp.

Two Whites Don't Make A Black

It is not possible for two pure white dogs to produce a litter of black pups, according to a judge in a recent litigation suit.

A wealthy 74-year-old woman owned a beautiful white poodle called Caro. She paid £100 to a breeder in Wales to have Caro mated with his pedigree white poodle. She drove Caro up to his stud in Wales and the dogs were 'introduced'; but there was no interest on the part of either party.

After the first meeting, the woman told the court that she had been asked to wait outside the kennel and the breeder took the two dogs into a clipping room.

He came out of the clipping room 30 minutes later and said that the mating had occurred. Nine weeks after the breeding session Caro gave birth to six jet black puppies.

The owner of the stud, after testifying that the two white poodles had mated, suggested to the court that Caro had been unfaithful to her pedigree.

The judge said that this was unlikely as the dog was kept, alone, behind two six-foot fences. He awarded the woman more than £1,000 damages as black poodles have less than half the market value of white ones.

★   ★   ★   ★

. . . . .There's a South American earthworm that's over six feet long. . . . .

★   ★   ★   ★

Here Pet

Gator Bait of Houma, Los Angeles, California was slightly worried when her grandmother refused to listen to her worries that her baby daughter, who was at the crawling stage, might be injured by gran's pet. Grandma has had her pet for two years and it has complete freedom of the garden. She feeds him every day, plays with him affectionately and says that he would not hurt a fly. Gator is not convinced. You see Cajun, the pet, is a five foot long, sharp toothed ALLIGATOR.

Killed By A Bite

A fourteen-year-old cattleboy called Edward, who worked in Richmond, South Africa, was walking through the plantation one day when he tripped over what he thought was a rope. Seconds later he was horrified to see a huge python begin to coil itself around his legs.

The boy could do nothing as the snake coiled itself right up his legs and round his chest, crushing every ounce of air out of his lungs as it did so. As the horrendous coils circled towards his throat the boy realized that there was only one thing to do.

He managed to snap at the snake with his teeth. The first time the snake slipped out of the boy's mouth, but at the second attempt he got a good bite and managed to hold on.

The harder he bit, the less the snake squeezed. It stopped shaking its head and the boy chewed on. Eventually the snake stopped squeezing completely and slid to the ground. Dead.

Police were astonished a few minutes later when the boy calmly walked into the police station and told them what he had done. They refused to believe him until he took them outside and showed them the body of the snake with its head almost chewed off.

A Shaggy Dog Story

Neighbours of Ginete Franke in Cleveland, Ohio were distressed by the smell that often came from her house. 'It's only the dogs,' she would say reassuringly. 'I'll see to it.' But the stench got no better so residents called in the police. When police knocked on her door the smell was so overpowering that several policemen were sick. But Mrs Franke had been telling the truth – it was the dogs causing the smell – all 127 of them.

A Lot Of Litter

In 1944, an American foxhound called Lena began to give birth to a litter of pups. Her anxious owners watched with delight as the first pup emerged, then another, then another, then another, then another ... there were 23 altogether.

★　　★　　★　　★

. . . . .The eagle can see straight ahead, although its eyes are on the side of its head. . . . .

★　　★　　★　　★

A Secured Loan

The manager of a Detroit Bank was quite willing to lend the pretty woman sitting across the desk from him the $1,000 she requested, but had to ask for some security. 'No problem,' the prospective borrower replied. 'I'll be back in a moment.' A few minutes later she returned with the collateral – a 25-pound tiger cub called Tinker Bell. The woman was an animal trainer. The tiger cub was insured at Lloyds in London and she told the bank manager that the loan would be repaid from payments she received from people who rented the tiger cub. She got her loan.

Worm Eats Dog (Biscuits)

Researchers at Dublin University wanted to do some work that needed woodworms – plump ones. The only ones that were available were too thin so Dr Sean Thompson, leader of the team, fed them on dog biscuits. Within one month they had grown to twenty times the size of an average woodworm.

WOOF WOOF!

You've Heard Of Raining Cats And Dogs... But

In 1973 the villagers of Brignoles in France were astonished when there was a freak storm and thousands of toads fell out of the sky. They had been whisked up into the sky by a whirlwind which blew across their nearby breeding ground, and, having blown itself out, left the toads to fall to the ground over Brignoles.

The Word Of The Lord Spreads

A shark caught in Antigual waters was found to have some odd items in its stomach when local natives cut it open. There was a human skull, a pair of suede shoes, and a copy of the Gospel According to St John printed on polythene.

Birds VC

In the grounds of All-Hallows-by-the-Tower, in London, there is a strange memorial. It was dedicated in 1946 by the then vicar the Rev. P. B. Clayton, and was organized by a Miss Nancy Price.

The memorial takes the form of a small rowan tree trunk with forked branches set in a rough stone base which forms two pools for water. Between the branches at different heights are wooden troughs for crumbs to feed the birds. On its branches are carved wooden pigeons, canaries and sparrows.

The memorial is dedicated to the memory of the pigeons that died on active service during the Second World War. Apparently, in one operation 27,000 pigeons were used, and it was a pigeon that brought the first news of the fall of Tunis to the British Army Headquarters in North Africa.

★ ★ ★ ★

.............The dragonfly flies with its legs together forming a basket in which to capture insects that it eats while in the air..

Strange Tastes

Some dogs are said to take exception to postmen and other people who invade their territory. Others seem to develop fixations for motor car wheels and if off the leash, tend to chase them. But Otto, a bulldog in Virginia Beach, Vermont has something against skateboards. Woe betide any unaware boy or girl 'boarding through Otto's territory. His score so far: an uncountable number of boards – two broken arms, one fractured leg and a smashed kneecap – as well as quite a few bloody noses.

A Lion's Tale

Judson Brown, a zookeeper at Prospect Park in Brooklyn was attacked by a lion that had somehow managed to escape from its cage. The animal was mauling Mr Brown on the arm and hand and would undoubtedly have killed him were it not for quick-thinking Dennis McCarthy who happened to be passing the bloody scene. He simply whipped off his belt and beat the lion once across its back. The lion was so astonished that it stopped its attack and the lucky zookeeper was pulled free.

★   ★   ★   ★

. . . .*An American airliner flying at 20,000 feet over South America was hit by a condor.* . . . .

★   ★   ★   ★

Cat And Mouse

The family cat of M. and Mme Blond of Nevers in France was a happy, peace-loving animal who would never do any harm. Until one night when the family were seated around the television watching a Tom and Jerry cartoon. All of a sudden, during a sequence when Tom was chasing Jerry, the cat went berserk and attacked the family. When police were called, the cat was a spitting ball of fury being kept at bay by M. Blond with the aid of a chair. The unfortunate animal refused to calm down and had to be destroyed.

In A Word

.... *Being matters of a verbal, linguistic or etymological nature................,.........................*

Well Named

A Montreal bank-clerk, appropriately named Gerry Cash, fell in love with one of his attractive colleagues and was delighted when she accepted his proposal of marriage. So Mr and Mrs Cash now work side by side in the bank. She was actually quite relieved. Her married name, Cash, is much more acceptable than her maiden name – Crook.

Tea-Clipping Whisky

One of the most famous export brands of Scotch whisky is named Cutty Sark – all because the patron of a lunch club in, London won a bet.

Over three hundred years ago the firm of Berry Brothers and Rudd opened a coffee mill at St James's Street in London. (It is still there.) They also served fine Scotch whisky to such famous people as Lord Byron and Beau Brummel – the whisky was simply called Berry Bros Scotch Whisky.

One day in the 1870s when members were having a luncheon party it was suggested that a more suitable name could be found for the popular drink. One of the guests had just won heavily on a race between some tea clippers coming back from India to England with their cargoes – the winner was called Cutty Sark.

The other guests gave this suggestion their unanimous approval, and an artist who was present immediately tore a sheet of yellow paper from his pocket and sketched the beautiful ship and her name. Both the name and the drawing are still used today.

Abuse Of Language

A New York surgeon was interviewed outside Belle Vue Hospital after an old lady of eighty-two had been knocked down while waiting for a bus, and had tragically lost her leg. The interviewer asked the surgeon if there was any likelihood of the limb being sewn back on to her body. 'No,' the surgeon replied. 'We have examined the lady and the leg and they are not candidates for reattachment.'

I Command It

People who bought an edition of the Bible printed in 1631 by Barker and Lucas were surprised (some may have been pleasantly so) when they came to the following verse in the Book of Exodus:

20:14 Thou shalt commit adultery.

The printers had inadvertently left out the word 'not'. The English monarch, Charles I, was horrified, recalled all 1,000 copies and fined the printers £3,000.

Revenge From Beyond The Grave

The sixteenth-century Countess of Seafield was not amused when a local clairvoyant known as the Brahan Seer, told her that her husband had a mistress in Perth. She was so angry that she ordered that the unfortunate man be boiled in tar. As he was about to be cast into the bubbling liquid, he prophesied that the line of Seafields would die out with a deaf and dumb girl, and that the estate would be inherited by a 'white-clothed lassie who would kill her sister.'

Two centuries later Francis Mackenzie, who was last in the line, was struck deaf and dumb. His eldest daughter, recently widowed, inherited the estate and arrived to claim her inheritance wearing white from head to toe. Later while she was out driving, the horses reared up and her sister was thrown from the carriage and died instantly.

★　　★　　★　　★

............*Salt was so valuable in Roman times that Julius Caesar paid his soldiers in salt rather than money. The Latin word for salt is 'sal', thus giving us the word 'salary'.*.......................................

★　　★　　★　　★

Sent To The Louis

Many people think that the traditional French method of executing criminals was named after Joseph Guillotin, who invented it. Wrong. It *was* named after him, but not because he invented it but because he was the man who recommended that a device for executing people swiftly and as painlessly as possible be developed. It was actually invented by Dr Antoine Louis and was originally called the *Louisette*. But somehow being sentenced to death by *Louisette* does not have the same sinister ring to it.

★   ★   ★   ★

. . . . *The Indian name for Lake Webster in Massachusetts is Chargogatmanchaugagochaubunagungamaug, which, when translated, means 'You fish on your side, we fish on our side, nobody fishes in the middle.'* . . . .

★   ★   ★   ★

There Are No Such Things As Sardines

When you buy a can of sardines you are not getting any particular kind of fish. Sardine is the name given to several different species of herring which are caught when young, and packed in flat tins for sale in shops and supermarkets around the world. In California the sardine is usually a young pilchard. In England it is usually the young of the Cornish pilchard and in Norway, sardines are normally sprats or brisling.

Sounds Painful

The Japanese words for 'four' and 'death' sound almost identical. So, too, do their words for 'nine' and 'suffering'. Because of any unfortunate confusions resulting from this, many hospitals in Japan do not have any wards numbered 4 or 9.

A Gobbledygook Explanation

The editor of the National Taxpayer's Union, an American organization that takes a keen interest in how the taxpayer's money is spent, is up in arms at a grant of $45,000 to the National Science Foundation. The latter august body want to study how the Caribbean lizard competes with birds and other lizards for food. They freely admit that the lizard has already been extensively studied but justify the grant as follows:

The Research is pertinent to applied ecology because the government of the Lesser Antilles is attempting to inventory its biotic wealth preparatory to the establishment of a cohesive national party policy.

Mr Eric Meltzer, the editor, said in reply, 'Instead of funding such a programme we should do basic research on what motivates bureaucrats to fund such unnecessary projects.'

The Most Famous Cook In America Doesn't Exist And Never Did!

The manufacturers of Gold Medal flour decided to publicize their product by publishing a picture puzzle in several national magazines. When it was solved, the puzzle showed a scene depicting customers carrying sacks of Gold Medal flour to their lorries.

More than 30,000 people sent in the completed puzzle and, along with the answer, many of them sent in questions about baking with the flour. Each letter received a personal reply but the question of who was to sign it soon arose. A well-loved secretary-director of the company had recently retired, so it was decided to use her surname and a cosy-sounding first name was then added.

Since then the name has been seen on cookery books, household hint books, recipe cards, and there is a department of five specially-trained correspondents, 23 trained home economists using five special kitchens who constantly test products and create new recipes bearing it. They receive between four and five thousand letters every month as well as 1,200 guests from all over the world.

The name that was made up to answer all these questions so long ago is now one of the most famous in all America – Betty Crocker.

★   ★   ★   ★

. . . .*'I would rather,' declared a distinguished academic, when addressing a gathering in Kentucky in 1956, 'sit at the feet of the Lord than dwell in the house of the mighty.' Whereupon he promptly died.* . . . .

★   ★   ★   ★

. . . .*In 1945 the bursar of Magdalen College, Oxford was named Cook, the cook was named Butler and the butler was called Chamberlain.* . . . .

★   ★   ★   ★

Odd Censorship

The Turkish government was very sensitive about allowing reports of foreign events to appear uncensored in the newspapers. When the American President William MacKinley was assassinated in 1901, it was reported that he had died of anthrax, but this was nothing compared to the official version of the deaths of the King and Queen of Serbia who were assassinated in 1903. Turkish readers were very sorry to read that their Royal Highnesses had died of indigestion.

A Curate's Egg

Samuel Johnson, the English lexicographer, was once sent a manuscript from an unknown author and asked for his advice. The great man wrote back:

Your manuscript is both good and original. But the part that is good is not original, and the part that is original is not good.

A Dash Of Sandys, Sir?

Over one hundred years ago a British nobleman, Sir Duncan Sandys, returned from India where he had been Governor of Bengal. He brought back with him the recipe for a sauce made of several Indian spices.

When he returned home he sought out two chemists near where he lived, gave them the recipe and asked them to make some for his own use. As a lavish host, Sir Duncan entertained often and well and the sauce became much talked about.

Eventually the two chemists asked his permission to manufacture the sauce on a small scale for sale. Sir Duncan gave his permission and today the sauce is used throughout the world, still made to the treasured secret recipe. The two chemists decided to name the sauce after the county in which they lived. Worcestershire. And the chemists' names? Mr John W. Lee and his partner, William Perrins.

121

Thank Goodness She Wasn't Called Boneta

The word 'money' comes to us from the Latin. The ancient Romans used to store their gold and silver in the temple of the goddess Juno Moneta - hence 'money'. Just think; had she been called Juno Boneta, we would be walking around with bunnies in our pockets.

A Lot To Do In Such A Short Time

A North of England newspaper once advised its readers that if news of a nuclear attack being launched broke, they should paint their windows with a mixture of whitewash and curdled whey in order to deflect dangerous rays, and soak their furniture in a solution of borax and starch to prevent fire. What the readers were expected to do with the remainder of the four-minute-warning, the paper did not say. Try the crossword, perhaps?

You're Not Going To Believe This

Scott Raoul Sor-Lokken has a pretty daughter called Snow Owl. At least that's what she's called by her family and friends. But, her real name is something very different.

Scott was so upset by government bureaucracy when he filed his tax return the year that Snow Owl was conceived that he decided to throw a spanner into the works and cause some confusion when he registered her name.

At first the Washington State registry office refused to accept the name, but Scott insisted and said that that was the name he had chosen for his daughter and that was the name he wanted on her birth certificate.

He was so adamant that the department relented – very reluctantly.

Not surprising really when you read Snow Owl's official name – Snowowlwolfeschlegelsteinhausenbergerdorffvoralternwarenge wissenhaftschaferswessenschafewarenwohlgepflegeundsorfg- faltigkeitbeschutzenvonangreifendurchahrraubgierigfeiene- welchevoralternzwolftausendjahresvorandieerscheinenvanderer- steerdemenschderraumschiffgebrauchlichtalsseinursprung- vonkraftgestartseinlangefahrthinzwischensternartigraumaufder- suchenachdiesternwelchegenabtbewohnbarplanetenkreise- drehensichundwohinderneurassevonverstandigmenscklich- keitkinntefortplannenundsicherfreuenanlebenslanglichfreude- undrehemitnichteinfurchtvorangreifenvonandererintelligent- geschopfsvonhinzwischensternartigraum Ellen Georgianna Sor-Lokken.

A Bad Choice Of Words

In Hoilywood, during the shooting of a film, it used to be customary for parties of sightseers to be allowed into the set when shooting was finished for the day. They could wander around and, if any of the actors were there, could feel free to approach them. One famous English actor was approached by such a party. His latest film, *Witness for the Prosecution*, had just been released. An effusive American lady walked up to him and gushingly said, 'Oh Mr ...... I just loved your performance in *Witness for the Prostitution*.'

Enigma Variations

.................Being matters of a supernatural,
coincidental or mysterious nature.........................

The Curse Of Tutankhamun

Most people scoff at the idea of curses coming true, but the events that followed the opening of Tutankhamun's tomb by Howard Carter in 1922 may make them think twice before laughing.

The story of the curse began when the last man climbed out of the tomb. It is said that a sudden sandstorm blew up and that the men in the party saw a hawk, the ancient royal symbol of Egypt, fly overhead.

Local Egyptians took this to mean that the spirit of the dead king had left his tomb, cursing those who had opened it. Five months later, the man who had financed the expedition, Lord Carnarvon, was bitten on the cheek by a mosquito. Normally nothing too serious! But the bite became infected and Carnarvon caught pneumonia and died in an Egyptian hospital.

At the precise moment of his death all the lights in Cairo went out, and thousands of miles away at the Carnarvon mansion in Hampshire, his dog began to howl – and died that night. Doctors who examined the mummified body of Tutankhamun reported that he had a small depression on his cheek, just like a mosquito bite, in exactly the same spot where Carnarvon had been bitten.

Strange deaths also befell many people who visited the tomb. Lord Carnarvon's half brother died of a burst appendix. An Egyptian prince whose family claimed descent from the pharaohs was murdered in London and his brother committed suicide. An American railway tycoon caught a cold while at the tomb and died of pneumonia.

The man who helped Howard Carter to catalogue the items found in the tomb committed suicide, and a few months later his father jumped to his death from a balcony at his London flat. There was an alabaster vase from the tomb in the room that he jumped from.

In 1966 the government of Egypt agreed to lend the treasures to France for an important exhibition. The Director of Antiquities fought against the decision, for he had dreamed that he would die if he allowed the treasures to go out of Egypt. When he left the last meeting, still trying to make the authorities change their minds, he was knocked down by a car and died two days later.

And Howard Carter who was the first man into the tomb? He died – of natural causes – in 1939.

Not Another One

In 1982 Helen Patterson won the £983 jackpot in a Scottish bingo club. Her husband won £13.00 on a fruit machine on the same night. A few days later, Mrs Patterson had three small bingo wins and her husband took another £20.00 from the fruit machine. A few weeks later Helen had another win, taking their joint winnings up to £1,900.

A few days later Robert Patterson, no relation, won £70.00 and several days after that his wife hit the jackpot with a bingo win of £853. The next day, she had four more small wins.

Later in the same week, an elderly lady was being presented with a cheque for £500 which she had just won. The manager jokingly asked her if her name was Patterson. The lady looked completely taken aback. 'No', she said. 'But it used to be. It was my maiden name.'

★　　★　　★　　★

. . . . In Redruth, Cornwall in 1906, two cars crashed into each other. Nothing unusual in that you may say – but they were the only two cars in the town at the time. . . . .

★　　★　　★　　★

. . . . The author of several books promoting clean living, including one called Nutrition for Health, *died of malnutrition. . . . .*

★　　★　　★　　★

Where Exactly Are We?

Walpole in Somerset is a tiny hamlet whose residents are up in arms against the local council. The hamlet was not listed on the last official census and is not on any maps. The postal address is Dunball, a nearby village. Ecclesiastically it is in the parish of Pawlett. Telephone numbers for the hamlet are coded under Puriton and it has recently been earmarked as an official rubbish tip.

An Unfair Fare

An Athenian taxi driver was more than a little surprised when the man he had stopped to pick up gave him his own address as his destination. The taxi driver did not say anything, but drove the passenger as requested. He got out of the car and let himself into the driver's house with a key. A few minutes later, the driver crept into his house and found his passenger and his wife making love. Out of the thousands of taxis in Athens, he would have picked that one.

Home Sweet Home

A Margate couple were in Wales on holiday. They decided to take a day trip on a British Rail Mystery Tour. As the train travelled towards its secret destination, the countryside became more and more familiar and the couple realized that they were about to arrive at their own home town.

Too Close For Comfort

On April 14, 1912, the 'unsinkable' *Titanic* struck an iceberg on her maiden voyage. It was packed with rich passengers, many of whom lost their lives as there were too few lifeboats to accommodate them all.

In 1898 a novel was published, called *Futility*, by journalist Margan Robertson.

It was about an unsinkable liner sailing from Southampton on her maiden voyage. Full of rich passengers, it struck an iceberg and sank killing many of those on board. The name of the ship in Robertson's novel was *Titan*.

Six years before *Futility* was published W.T. Stead, a well-known reporter, wrote a short story which also amazingly foreshadowed the sinking of the *Titanic*. Stead was one of the 1,513 who died when the great ship sank.

Twenty-three years after the *Titanic* went down, a young seaman called William Reeves was standing watch on a steamer bound from Tyneside to Canada.

The water was calm and there was no sign of any icebergs, but Reeves couldn't help but worry about what had happened to the *Titanic*, which had gone down in similar circumstances, and he wanted to shout a warning. The only thing that prevented him from doing so was the ribbing that his shipmates would give him.

Suddenly he remembered the date, April 14. It was his birthday.

Not only that, but it was the date that the *Titanic* sank – the very day that Reeves had been born.

Unable to stop himself he shouted a warning and the ship came to a halt a few yards away from a huge iceberg that loomed high above the ship.

The ship's name? *The Titanian*.

A Strange Premonition

A Gottenburg seaman often dreamt that he would die on his fiftieth birthday. The day came and he was happy to survive it – so happy that he gave a delayed birthday party to celebrate the fact that his dream had not come true. Unfortunately he got exceedingly drunk, had a heart attack and died.

Family Purse-uit

Alexi Sogmorov was cleaning the roads in Moscow one day when he found a purse with some money in it.

Being honest, he decided to return it to the owner whose address, but no name, was in the purse.

He was more than a little surprised when the door was opened by his sister Svetlana whom he had not seen for fourteen years.

What Happened To Them?

In 1858 a group of 18 Englishmen landed in Roanoke Island near the coast of North Carolina. Encouraged by Sir Walter Raleigh's example of two centuries before, they built a fort and houses, and planted crops. But hostile Indians made life impossible for them and they were forced to return home. The following year, another group re-settled on the island. After a few weeks the leader of the group, John White, sailed back to England to get more provisions. When he returned, all he found was a mysterious word carved on a tree:

CROATOAN

There was absolutely no sign of any of the settlers.

Well Oil Be Blowed

A bomber crew who happened to be carrying a chaplain among its numbers ran out of fuel and was forced to land on a Japanese-held island in the Pacific ocean. The crew resigned themselves to the fact that they would be captured and imprisoned by their Japanese enemies. The chaplain, a firm believer in the power of prayer, knelt down and asked his God to help them.

The next morning one of the crew felt a strong compulsion that he should go and take a walk down the beach. When he did so he found a huge drum of aviation fuel bobbing in the waves of the incoming tide. He ran back to the rest of the men and got them to help him carry the oil back to the plane. A few minutes later the bomber took off and returned to base.

They took note of the name on the drum and when they were safe they made inquiries about it. It turned out that the fuel had been part of a cargo that had been thrown overboard from an American barge after a Japanese attack. All the other drums had been lost, but this one had floated for over 1,000 miles past more than twenty other islands and miraculously turned up where it was sorely needed.

★　　★　　★　　★

.............Residents of Panther, West Virginia swear they know when a fire is about to break out because they see Big Red, the fire truck, racing down the street – which is strange, as Big Red went out of service several years ago and sits rusting and unable to move in the Volunteer Fire Department.......................................

★　　★　　★　　★

A Lot Of Coincidence

At an auction to raise funds for the Society for the Preservation of Rural Wales, a friend of Baroness White the organizer, decided to bid for five machine tapestries showing views of Venice and London.

He was surprised when he got the lot for £50.00. He had decided to spend more than that in aid of what he considered was a good cause, but everything else he bid for went for more than he was prepared to pay.

He was just about to leave when he saw two bottles of his favourite wine, a 1955 Gevrey Chambertin, were about to go under the hammer. His bid was accepted and he returned home quite happy with all he had bought.

The next morning he telephoned the Baroness to thank her for a pleasant evening and to tell her what he had bought.

'How very peculiar,' said Lady White. 'I was staying with friends last week and told them about the auction. They insisted on giving me something for it – five machine tapestries of Venice and London and two bottles of 1955 Gevrey Chambertin.'

131

Mr Otis Regrets...

One cold, blustery night towards the end of the last century, the British Ambassador to France, Lord Dufferin was visiting Ireland. One night he was unable to sleep. He left his bed and drew back the curtains from the window to see if the strong winds were doing any damage to the well-kept gardens. He was startled to see someone carrying a coffin across the lawn. He tapped loudly on the window and the man turned round. He had the most hideous face Lord Dufferin had ever seen – 'as if', he said to his wife, 'a long dead corpse had risen from the grave.'

A few years later Dufferin was back in Paris and had to go to a diplomatic reception in the Grand Hotel, which had recently installed one of the new-fangled lifts. He went to enter the lift and drew back in horrified amazement. The operator had the same face as the man he had seen running across the lawn some years before. The terrified lord drew back from the lift and decided to walk up the stairs.

A few seconds later there was a resounding crash as the cable snapped and the lift crashed to the basement. Everyone in it was killed – including the lift attendant.

Lightning Strikes

In Canada, during a fierce storm in 1934, the tombstone of an officer who had served in the First World War was shattered by a bolt of lightning. The unfortunate officer had been invalided out of the Canadian Army after being struck by lightning in 1918. Six years later he was struck by another flash while fishing, and his right side was paralysed. He recovered and two years later was taking a walk through a park when ... this time paralysing him for good. The gods must have had it in for him.

What A Coincidence

A Derbyshire lady and her husband were motoring south one day when they stopped at a motorway lay-by to rest. They got out of the car and fell into conversation with another couple. The second man happened to mention that a few months before he had lost his wallet containing credit cards, cash and other personal items. As he was talking he took the wallet out of his pocket and the astonished Derbyshire lady looked at it in amazement – it had been she who had found it and handed it in to the police, and the two couples lived more than 60 miles away from each other.

Dead Man's Tales

A Warwickshire builder was quite surprised to bump into a cousin he hadn't seen for some time in a pub. But not half as surprised as his cousin, who had been at the builder's funeral service in Dublin some time earlier. It turned out that former workmates had wrongly identified him as the victim of a car crash and had telephoned his family in Ireland. The family decided that rather than come over for the funeral, they would hold a mass for him there.

Hello, Father

Johann van Vliet, a Dutch tourist, was on holiday in Austria when his car broke down just outside Innsbruck. A local farmer's wife kindly stopped her car and offered him a lift to the nearest garage. It turned out that she was his daughter who had run away from home 23 years earlier.

A Ghostly Experience

Nell Wood of Redwood City, California, swears that the following story is true.

She woke up one morning with her stomach in knots. She was certain that something awful was going to happen and the feeling stayed with her all day.

When she went to bed that night she had a strange dream. In her dream her sister came to her and told her that there had been an accident. Two had been critically injured and one only slightly. Nell did not know what her sister meant by 'two' and 'one', but she sensed that her mother was involved. At that time her mother lived three thousand miles away.

The next day Nell's sister telephoned and told her that their mother had had a fall.

'She's broken her pelvic bone, her hip and the small bone in the leg. The small bone is not critical but the other two are.'

Nell's dream flooded back to her and she understood the meaning of the 'two' and the 'one'.

A few weeks later, Nell was lying in bed thinking about her mother's accident and how much she would like to visit her; she closed her eyes and dropped off to sleep.

She dreamed that she was in her mother's bedroom, standing at the bottom of the sleeping woman's bed. She did not want to waken her mother, but the old lady opened her eyes, smiled at Nell and went back to sleep.

The next morning her mother telephoned. She said she had dreamed in the night that Nell had been in her bedroom wearing a pale pink nightgown.

Nell was stunned, because she *had* been wearing a pale pink nightgown that night – a new one that her mother had never seen, and a colour she had never worn before.

A Good Gamble

Mr George Epp, a former policeman with Atlantic City Police Department quit the force because of his gambling debts. He felt it was giving the police a bad name, so he took a job as a taxi-driver to give himself time to get over his addiction. He worked hard to pay off the $25,000 he owed his creditors, but still found it hard to stop dicing with Lady Luck. Just as well. In the Atlantic City Casino one night in November 1982 he put some coins into a slot machine, pulled the handle and came out $1,250,000 richer.

A Tale Of Pearls

Two American women were on holiday in Britain, spending most of their time cycling from place to place, exploring the countryside and looking for inexpensive mementoes to take home.

They decided to go to Newhaven and found a cheap hotel to stay in overnight.

While wandering through the streets they came across a little junk shop and went in to buy some trinkets. The owner tried to sell them a little Bible and when this did not satisfy them, he picked up a string of beads which was hanging from a nail. The girls thought that these were just what they wanted and bought them for one shilling.

When they returned to London, they decided to have the beads re-strung as the cord was very frayed, so they took them to a jeweller.

The assistant said he would do the job that day and the beads would be ready the following morning.

When they returned to collect them, the jeweller asked them to step into his private office, where he introduced them to a stranger. The girls noticed their beads lying on the desk. They had been cleaned and polished and looked very beautiful.

The stranger, it turned out, was from the British Museum and was anxious to buy the beads from the two Americans. They had, he explained, belonged to Mary Queen of Scots, and had been missing ever since she was executed.

The beads were, in fact, a magnificent string of black pearls.

It Is Easier For A Rich Man...

A Shanghai millionaire, Woo Tai Ling, had a most disturbing dream one night. He dreamed that he was too overloaded with money to slip through the narrow gates into heaven. The next morning he gave all his money away and took a job in a market as an ordinary porter.

★　　★　　★　　★

.............In 1902 St Pierre in Martinique was totally destroyed and 40,000 people killed when Mount Pele erupted. The only survivor was a prisoner who was being kept in an underground cell. No-one knows how he got out..

★　　★　　★　　★

An Unfortunate Coincidence

Herr Keelsch of Seigen in West Germany made his living out of emptying cesspits – and, not unnaturally, after a day's work did not exactly smell of roses and violets. He drove around the town in a van which advertised his telephone number in large numbers. This so angered the makers of a certain well-known *eau de Cologne* that they took him to court to make him remove the offending numbers. As Herr Keelsch explained, it was not his fault that he had been given that famous number:

4711

Never Strike Twice?

In 1942 Roy Sullivan, a Park Ranger in Virginia, USA, lost a toe nail. Twenty-seven years later his eyebrows were damaged; the following year his left shoulder was burned and two years after that his hair was set on fire. It had grown again by the following year and then the same thing happened again. In 1976 his ankle was injured and in 1977 he suffered chest burns. The cause of all this misfortune? Lightning! All in all he has been struck seven times – and most people say that lightning never strikes in the same place twice. Tell that to the rangers.

Eccentricity Generating

.... *Being matters of a kind concerning
freaks and eccentricities of behaviour or occurrence..*

Don't Meddle With The Ref

During a game between Catanzaro and Palermo, the score was one goal each when the home side, Catanzaro, had two penalties disallowed by the referee.

When the final whistle blew, the referee was chased from the ground. Fortunately, he was a fast runner and managed to dash into a restaurant, where he called a waiter and ordered some soup, hoping to give his pursuers the slip.

Unfortunately, when his meal arrived, so too did the owner of the restaurant, who had just come back from the match.

Recognizing the referee, the angry proprietor ordered him from the restaurant, throwing the soup after him. The furious referee, however, managed to get his revenge.

He found a telephone and called the restaurant. He told the owner that he was the manager of the Catanzaro team and he was bringing his players there for something to eat. They would, he said, be arriving in about an hour.

He then telephoned the Catanzaro manager and claimed to be the restaurant owner.

He told the manager that he was so upset by the result and so convinced that the local side had won that he was inviting the entire team to eat at the restaurant for a few pence each. Come, he said, in about an hour.

The footballers duly arrived and ate and drank their way through the menu.

When they were presented with an enormous bill they went crazy and broke up the restaurant.

The restaurant manager and the football manager had such a fight that the furious footballer was jailed for assault.

Quicker Clearance

A cinema manager once wrote to the *Daily Worker* (now the *Morning Star*) deploring the fact that the practice of playing the National Anthem was being phased out. He claimed that those who were lucky enough managed to leave the cinema before it started, and those left behind moved off more quickly, thus clearing the cinema in a shorter time than on occasions when 'The Queen' was not played.

Turn Up The Sound

A Los Angeles record company has produced an album entitled 'The Best of Marcel Marceau'. Each side has twenty minutes of M. Marceau in performance, followed by applause. M. Marceau is, of course, a well-known mime artist and never utters a word during his act.

A Short Time For 'A Long Way...'

The famous song 'It's a Long Way to Tipperary' was written by two friends, Jack Judge and Harry J. Williams, as the result of a bet. They were challenged by a group of actors to write a song and perform it the same day. So they sat down in a pub and did just that.

The song is still popular today, over seventy years later, especially in pubs!

★   ★   ★   ★

. . . . .When a distraught widow saw a pair of bright, white false teeth grinning up at her from the funeral urn, she knew there was something wrong – her husband had never had false teeth in his life. . . . .

★   ★   ★   ★

If Mr Marconi Had Only Known

The proud mother surveyed her children. There were eighteen of them – fourteen of whom had different fathers, and all of whom had been born after the mother had left her husband. The woman said that she neither smoked nor drank and that her only relaxation was the radio.

Over What Sea?

A North London man asked an official at Golders Green Crematorium if he could have the ashes of his deceased mother. He was asked where he intended taking them, and when he told the official, he was asked to pay £2, the usual amount if ashes were to be taken overseas.

The man was slightly puzzled and contacted the Home Office to be told that, under their regulations, the attendant had been quite correct.

'Scotland,' he was told, 'is officially overseas.'

The official could not say which sea it was over, but he had to stick by the ruling and charge the fee.

Small Is Beautiful

One of the most successful spies of the French Revolution was a thirty-two-year-old man who devised a novel way of slipping through enemy lines. He was so small that he was dressed up as a baby and was simply carried past unsuspecting guards by a female colleague.

A Cleveland Duel

A long-standing feud between two men who lived in a Cleveland apartment house came to a head one day.

Both men returned to their separate abodes and came back into the hallway each brandishing an antique pistol. Standing five feet apart, they took aim and fired, again, again and again – a total of six shots each.

When the police arrived, there were bullet holes all over the hallway but both men were alive. The detective in charge said that one of the contestants needed a stick to prop himself up while firing and the other had trouble seeing as he suffered from glaucoma in the eye. One of the men was 76 and the other was 77.

When did all this happen? Not during the last century as you may imagine, but in May 1981.

A Taxing Problem

Arthur Cox has one of the strangest food shops in Britain. He refuses to sell anything that carries VAT. He won't sell chocolate biscuits, but will sell chocolate-covered cakes. Cat food is not sold, but tinned fish is. But Mr Cox *is* registered for VAT. That way he can claim back the VAT on items that he buys for the shop, such as paper bags and till rolls. So the VAT man must pay him, without getting anything back from him.

High Speed Shopping

Villagers who live in the Oxfordshire hamlet of Finstock have to be the fastest shoppers in the world. Most of them do their shopping in the nearby town of Charlesbury, three miles away. The first available bus, run by the Oxford-South Midland Bus Company arrives in Charlesbury at 11.38 am. The last bus from Charlesbury back to Finstock leaves at 11.41 am. This gives the Finstock villagers three minutes to do their shopping.

Wednesday, Thursday, Thursday, Saturday...

In 1147, Pope Eugene III visited Paris. He entered the city on a Friday, although he knew that by doing so the people would be unable to celebrate his arrival, as Friday was an official day of fasting for all Roman Catholics. So a Papal decree was issued to say that that particular Friday was a Thursday.

Water Baby

Many people have managed to swim a mile, so there's nothing unusual in Simon Broadhurst doing it. Only it took him two hours – he was only three years old when he did his marathon swim at Saddleworth Baths near Manchester.

Excuse Me But That Painting's Hanging Upside Down

A painting by the famous French impressionist painter, Manet, was lent to the New York Museum of Modern Art for an important exhibition, which ran from April through October. The painting showed a village reflected in a small lake. It was only after the exhibition had finished that one of the museum attendants realized that it had been hung upside down. No one had noticed, although many people had stopped in front of the painting and admired Manet's skill.

★　★　★　★

..............In late 1981 a teenage couple who were anxious to get into the record books embraced each other and began to kiss – five days, twelve hours later they broke off..

★　★　★　★

144

Coals To Newcastle

Abu Dhabi is one of the most desert-covered countries in the world. No matter where you look there is sand, sand and more sand. Yet a British firm once took an order to export 1,800 tons of sand to them.

The Rich Get Richer

Sutton Place was the home of J. Paul Getty, one of the richest of twentieth century oil millionaires. Weekend guests to his sumptuous home were astonished to find telephone boxes installed for their use. Despite his enormous wealth, Getty hated the thought of paying for other people's calls.

For Love of Guam

Yokoi Shoichi was stationed on the island of Guam when the Japanese surrendered to the Americans in 1945. Either no one told him or he refused to believe that the Imperial Japanese Army was capable of defeat, but for the next 27 years he lived in the jungle, eating small mammals and berries. He was found in 1972 and was returned to Japan.

A few years later he married and took his bride on honeymoon. Back to Guam.

One, Two, Three, Four...

Young Master Drew, a schoolboy in Waterloo, Iowa, ran home one day and told his mother, Martha, an amazing piece of information that he had learned that day in school. It was impossible, his teacher had said, to count up to one million. Martha Drew did not believe this, so she sat down at her typewriter and began to type out every number from one to one million. Five years and 2,473 sheets of paper later, she finished.

I HOPE YOU PASSED HER. SHE'S DRIVING THE CRANE!

A Long Way To Go For A Funeral

Mr and Mrs Richard Selley of Houston in Texas had almost forgotten that they had a wealthy cousin, until he died and left them one million dollars. Unfortunately, there was one condition they had to fulfil before they got the money – they had to arrange to have their benefactor buried on the moon.

The Gullible Burmese

There are many famous confidence trick stories ranging from shifty Frenchmen selling the Eiffel Tower, to the imposter who fooled the Albanians into believing that he was their king (for three days), but Lim Bim Sung, a Burmese man, came up with a winner. He convinced several people in Rangoon that he had bought an old American rocket and was organizing holidays on the moon. He was arrested as one potential customer was actually handing over the money for the fare.

★　★　★　★

. . . . *It took Austrian Johann Hurlinger 55 days to walk the 871 miles from Vienna to Paris. Mind you, he was walking on his hands all the way*. . . . .

Have I Passed Then?

The unfortunate examiner who saw a nervous woman learner driver through her driving test in Guildford in 1969 ended up on the roof of the car along with the woman when she drove into the River Wey. The shocked examiner was sent home before he had told the driver if she had passed or failed her test. Ever-hopeful, the woman asked if she had passed and was told with remarkable British reserve that no one knew, as the examiner had not told anyone before he went home.

Distracting Credit

In the USA it is very common for sales assistants to check a customer's credit balance whenever a credit card is offered in payment. The assistant simply punches the card number into a counter computer terminal and the amount of credit available flashes up on the VDU. An ill-tempered queue was once formed in a shop called Broadway Bazaar in, where else, Broadway, New York. A female customer handed over ten credit cards until the cashier found one that had a sufficient balance left in order to pay for her purchases.

Long way away, a Texan woman found a novel way around the problem. Wearing only the briefest of bikinis to cover her shapely figure, she spent a morning in a large Dallas store paying by credit card, choosing youngish male assistants to serve her. It was only after she had run up a bill of over £1,000 that any of the men bothered to check her non-existent credit-worthiness – their eyes were obviously elsewhere.

★　★　★　★

. . . . An American woman insured her husband's life so that, if he died before she did, her lifestyle would not change too radically. Some lifestyle – when he died the insurance company paid up $18,000,000. . . . .

A Close Shave

Robert Hardie was anxious to publicize the barber shop he opened in London in 1909. He persuaded a friend to be shaved by him in public. The friend agreed and Hardie gave him a clean shave in 29 seconds – blindfolded.

A Fortune From Nothing

For their seven-year run on Broadway, which began in 1896 the Cherry Sisters earned $1,000 per week. When the show finished, although they had lived well during the run, they had managed to save $200,000. Their act? They played a sketch that was so bad it had to be acted behind a wire screen to avoid the rotten tomatoes and vegetables that were thrown at them every night. People were happy to pay, simply to bombard them.

I NEVER MISSED A SHOW EXCEPT THE TIME I WRENCHED MY THROWING ARM!

Quite A Bargain

The Russians first colonized Alaska in the 1780s but by the 1850s many Americans and Canadians had settled there, too. The Russians offered to sell the area to the Americans and agreed to take $7.3 million for it. That works out at around two cents an acre. At first the Americans thought the Secretary of State who had negotiated with the Russians was mad and called Alaska 'Seward's Folly' after him. But when gold, and later, oil were discovered there in huge quantities they changed their minds quite quickly.

Blow It

Susan Montgomery, an American schoolgirl, decided to blow a huge bubble with her gum. She chewed and chewed until she felt that it was just the right consistency. She began to blow and stopped when the bubble had reached a diameter of 19¼ inches.

Multiple Votes

Bessie Braddock, the tough but well-respected member for Liverpool Central, often told the story of driving through her constituency one polling day when her car had to stop at traffic lights. One of her constituents recognized her and knocked on the window. Mrs Braddock dutifully wound it down to be told by the woman that she was a life-long admirer and had voted for her, as usual. Bessie thanked the woman. 'Don't mention it,' said the Liverpudlian, 'in fact I voted for you three times. Two of my friends are ill, so I just took their cards to their polling stations and voted for you, just in case.'

Fortunately Mrs Braddock's majority was large enough for her not to have to worry about these three votes robbing her opponent of victory. But had it been in Ilkeston during the 1931 general election, three votes would have made all the difference, for the majority with which Abraham Flint was returned to Westminster was two.

Live Long, Live Loudly

Every year, the townsfolk of Montforte d'Alba in Piedmont hold a free-style Shouting Festival. In 1982, 2,000 people were in the audience enjoying watching and listening to lusty youngsters screaming at the tops of their voices to see who could register the loudest and most piercing yell.

A ripple of sympathetic laughter spread through the audience when an old man was helped on to the platform. Their laughter turned to cheers when he registered a scream of 124 decibels on the phonometer – equivalent to the noise a jet aeroplane makes on landing. The winner was ninety years of age.

Sweet Revenge

Carlo Gamba left home in southern Italy in 1913 when he was twenty-three. He never returned to Italy and never saw his family again. He worked as a shoe black in a San Francisco railway station. He worked seven days a week and most nights. Carlo never married, never smoked or drank, saved every penny he could and invested what he had wisely.

In 1962, he learned that his brother, Giuseppe, had sold the family home in Italy for $1,000. Carlo did not receive a penny from the sale. He neither said a word about it, nor did he forgive.

When he died in 1982, Carlo had amassed a fortune of $500,000. Giuseppe heard this news with delight, but the smile on his face did not last long. Instead of the vast fortune he expected to receive, Giuseppe got exactly $5.

The will read, 'I leave all my money except five dollars to the town of Verbicaro (his home town) to build a hospital. These five dollars I leave to Giuseppe so that he can buy a drink and remember that he should never have sold the family house without my consent.'

★   ★   ★   ★

. . . .*The owner of a hotel in Chippenham, England, has a unique collection of drinks bottles. The contents are never sold in his hotel – the bottles are miniatures – all 19,000 of them.* . . . .

Foiled

Mithradates, king of a long-forgotten realm, attempted to make himself immune to poisons by taking increasingly large doses of toxic substances. It is ironic therefore that when he was defeated by his enemies, the Romans, he tried to commit suicide by taking poison. None of the poisons available did the trick so he had to ask a soldier to hold a sword for him, and he killed himself by running into it.

★   ★   ★   ★

............The name Billy Jones is not to be found in any of the record books, although one day in May 1955, at Louisiana, he ran the hundred yards in nine seconds, smashing every previous record. Unfortunately, when officials checked the distance, they found that the track was ten yards short.......................................

★   ★   ★   ★

An Odd Hobby

A man who works for Hertfordshire Social Services Committee has a very strange hobby. He traces twins who have no idea that they have twin brothers or sisters.

It all started more than twenty years ago when he became involved in the case of a boy who had been taken into care. He discovered that the child had been adopted and, before the boy left care, he said that his mother had told him he was one of a pair of twins. The boy went off to sea and the interested social worker decided to find out if this was true. He located the adoption society who put him in touch with the boy's grandmother. She knew where the other twin was. He had also gone off to sea.

Since then, the man has put 23 sets of twins in touch with each other. One set of twins found out that the only thing they liked to drink was advocaat and lemonade. Another set are both terrified of birds. Two boy twins turned up to meet each other wearing identical glasses, jackets and trousers, and other twins found that they lived within a mile of each other, drank in the same pubs and clubs and yet had never met until our intrepid investigator put them in touch with each other.

An Expensive Drink

In 1982, the Islay distillery of Bruichladdich decided to market a single malt whisky that had been maturing in oak sherry casks for fifteen years. They decided that such a fine old whisky should be treated with respect, so they commissioned Edinburgh crystal manufacturers to make special crystal decanters, plus a lock-fast Victorian-style tantalus, which holds two decanters of the precious liquid. The price of all this in the Italian shops where the 'cratur' was to be sold? The equivalent of £1,000. At normal pub measures that works out at £20 for a dram.

★　　★　　★　　★

. . . . A Portsmouth man who died recently left £250,000 in his will to . . . Jesus Christ, provided that he comes back to earth within the next twenty-one years. . . . . . .

★　　★　　★　　★

What A Shower

Some members of a Home Counties Soccer Club have complained to the London Football Association about one of their referees, who insists on taking a shower with them after the game. The referee, shapely Janet Walmsley, does not see what all the fuss is about. 'After all,' she says, 'I do keep my knickers on.'

A Close Run Thing

Willie Carson, the famous British jockey, was racing one day at Pontefract. He was happily leading on the rails, having made all the running. A furlong and a half from home he thought he heard something at his back and, glancing round, he saw the shadow of a horse coming up behind. Determined that he should not be beaten, he spurred on and was first past the post. He looked round and saw that the nearest horse was fifteen lengths behind – he had been racing his own shadow for the last part of the race.

How Have The Mighty Fallen

The Sri-Lanka tribe of Rodiya was once one of the mightiest on the island. They were in charge of collecting taxes and ensuring that whatever the king said was obeyed. One of their number was responsible for supplying the king's table with fresh game.

One day the king told his Rodiyan servant that he wanted freshly roasted venison for dinner. Unfortunately, deer was scarce in the forest and the hunters came home empty-handed. The terrified servant hit upon a substitute and the royal family pronounced the meal delicious until a human finger was found in the serving bowl.

The hunter was summoned before the furious king and confessed that he had slaughtered and cooked a human. He was instantly beheaded and, as punishment, all the Rodiyans were banished and denied all forms of work other than begging.

Although all this happened 1,500 years ago and the Sri-Lankan monarchy has long since died out, the Rodiyans still live by begging. The old royal decree has long been lifted, but the Rodiyans know no other way of life apart from that forced on them by the king.

Dance Of The Seven Veils — And Then Some

The vicar of a Sheffield parish was slightly perturbed when he heard that students at one of the local colleges were going to put on Oscar Wilde's famous play, *Salome*. The girl who was to play Salome heeded the vicar's warning about her role — for when she did the dance of the seven veils, she wore a flared skirt and tunic under her costume. Many of the men in the audience were slightly upset about this and did not applaud as Wildely as the happy vicar.

★   ★   ★   ★

. . . . Those who were lucky enough to see an early print of El Cid, an epic film set in twelfth-century Spain, were amused when a large truck was clearly visible on the horizon during one sweeping camera shot. . . . .

TOUR de FRANC
SOUP TO NUTS STAGE

. . . . In 1977 a certain Frenchman was feeling slightly peckish – so he ate a bicycle, every last nut and bolt of it. . . . .

★ ★ ★ ★

The Sausages Were Off

The foul smell that came from a Welwyn Garden City sausage skin factory so upset a local businessman that he went out and bought the entire works. It was only after he had done so that he discovered that the factory could only be used to manufacture certain things under a local by-law. The other uses included the boiling of blood, the breeding of maggots and the preparation of glue and manure.

154

Is The Old Way Best?

To try to teach her class of schoolchildren something about what life was like in Victorian England, a North London school teacher decided to put the clock back one hundred years. She raided the drama club wardrobe and found enough Victorian-style dresses for the girls to wear for one day and asked the boys to turn up wearing smart jackets, collars and ties.

When the teacher walked into the classroom on the morning of the lesson, the children all stood up and bade her good morning as rehearsed.

They then recited their tables in time to a metronome that had been installed in the classroom. Anyone who misbehaved was made to stand in the corner, a dunce's cap on his head. Lunch was served – a simple meal of gruel.

The pupils said it was the best day of school they had ever had and begged to repeat the experiment again and again – that is, apart from the lunch.

A Really Nervous Passenger

A Rotherham man had never flown before, but decided to fly to Bulgaria for a holiday. He boarded the 'plane and a few minutes later the engines roared into life and it began to taxi down the runway. It was then that he suddenly realized that in a few minutes he would be flying at supersonic speeds thousands of feet above the ground. He unfastened the seat belt and asked a stewardess to have the 'plane stopped. The girl tried to calm him down, but it was no good. The pilot took the 'plane back to the terminal and the man ran down the steps, rushed to get a taxi and went back to his house in Rotherham. What happened to his baggage, that's what I want to know?

★   ★   ★   ★

.............In 1910, the eccentric Polish aristocrat, the Princess Radzewill, drove a chariot pulled by a lion and a leopard. . . . .

★   ★   ★   ★

Help! My Baby's In There

Tony Stellato was only too pleased to help the hysterical lady who stopped him in the street, pointed to a blazing building and told him that her baby was trapped in the fire. He battled his way through a wall of smoke and flames and frantically searched for the child. But he could find nothing. He stumbled back into the garden, gasping for breath.

The lady pleaded with him again to go and find her baby, so he ran back into the conflagration, broke through a locked door, and still found nothing. Suddenly a blast of smoke hit him in the face and he began to lose consciousness. He stumbled outside and managed to make it into the fresh air before passing out. He was rushed to hospital and treated for severe smoke inhalation.

When he was fully recovered the doctors told him that he was a real hero, although they did not understand why he had risked his life to try to save a cat called 'Baby'.

It later turned out that the cat had left the house as soon as the fire had started.

Luckless Heirs

During the American Civil War, New York society was dazzled by a beautiful woman called Ida Mayfield. She married a congressman, Ben Wood, who showered her with money and jewels. When she travelled to Europe she was introduced to the Empress Eugénie of France. She danced in London with the Prince of Wales, and back home she entertained President Cleveland.

Then, in 1901, Ida mysteriously vanished. In 1931 the *New York Daily News* stated that she had been discovered living in a shabby state in New York's Herald Square Hotel. Her room looked like a hamster's cage. There were mountains of yellowed newspapers and hundreds of letters scattered across the floor. Trunks and boxes were stacked from ceiling to floor. Ida was blind and deaf and wore two of the hotel's towels held together by safety-pins as a dress.

She was pronounced to be mentally incompetent and made a ward of court. The judge ordered that the boxes be opened. They contained securities worth hundreds of thousands of dollars, as well as a magnificent emerald and diamond necklace of priceless value. But it was the nurse who came to look after Ida who made the real discovery.

Around the old woman's waist was a canvas and oilcloth pouch containing $500,000 in ten-thousand-dollar bills.

When this was taken from Ida, the shock was so much that she had a stroke and died, leaving no obvious heirs.

Soon every Mayfield in Louisianna seemed to have arrived in New York claiming to be a relation of Ida's. It took four years for the courts to make a decision – and when it was announced the Mayfields were horrified.

Ida Mayfield, the court decreed, had never existed. The woman who claimed to be her was, in fact, Ellen Walsh, the impoverished daughter of an immigrant textile worker. Though poor as a church mouse, Ellen had brains as well as beauty.

She borrowed a ballgown and journeyed to New York, adopting the name of Ida Mayfield when she arrived there. She soon became the toast of the town, after gate crashing a party in her one borrowed frock. Because she looked the part of a rich, elegant lady, fashionable clothes shops gave her credit, which was soon paid off when she married Ben Wood. Not even he knew the truth about his wife.

The fortune that she left was divided among a handful of descendants who were located after quite a search. They did not even know that their ancestor had ever existed.

★　　★　　★　　★

............Gary Trench of Phoenix, Arizona once sleepwalked to his place of work and did a three-hour shift packing toys before he woke.........................

★　　★　　★　　★

A Little Overdue

The librarian of Cincinnati Medical Library thought his eyes were deceiving him when he checked the return date of the book in front of him. It was due back in 1823 having originally been taken out by the great-grandfather of the returner. The fine of $2,646 was waived under the circumstances.

A Credit To The American Educational System

The US university system is slightly different from the British one. In order to graduate to the next year, students must build up a required number of credits. The classes are not necessarily academic.

At the University of Massachusetts, students are offered a class in ghosts and apparitions. At the University of Southern California, figure improvement is a credit subject popular among plump sorority girls.

At Hampshire College in Amhurst, frisbee-throwing is a credit subject, along with a study called extra-terrestrial intelligence, in which students are taught to develop languages that might be useful in communicating with alien beings who happen to land on earth. At UCLA, a credit course on nude photography was oversubscribed within minutes of opening for registration.

Long Distance Love Comes Expensive

Terry Jasper was quite pleased when his shy 19-year-old son, Damon, found a girlfriend. Although Damon never brought her home, he spent a lot of time on the telephone to her and Terry was pleased to see his son so happy.

What Dad did not know was that Damon's girlfriend, Donna, lived in Hong Kong. When the first bill came in after the romance ha started, Terry was horrified to read that it came to $6,000, compared with the usual $120. The collector then warned Terry that there was already $8,000 due on calls on the next bill.

Damon later said, 'All I wanted to do was get engaged. When Donna's dad took her to Hong Kong that was bad enough. But now my love life has turned into a terrible nightmare. How can I get married with Dad insisting I pay off every penny I owe him?'

Darn It

The Nizam of Hyderabad was one of the richest men in the world. His jewels alone were estimated to be worth £400 million, and they represented only a part of his vast fortune.

He had a retinue of thousands of servants, and yet he hated throwing clothes away. Whenever they were in danger of fraying or wearing out, he had them carefully darned.